Exploring the 3-D World

Other Redleaf Press Books by Rosanne Regan Hansel

Creative Block Play: A Comprehensive Guide to Learning through Building

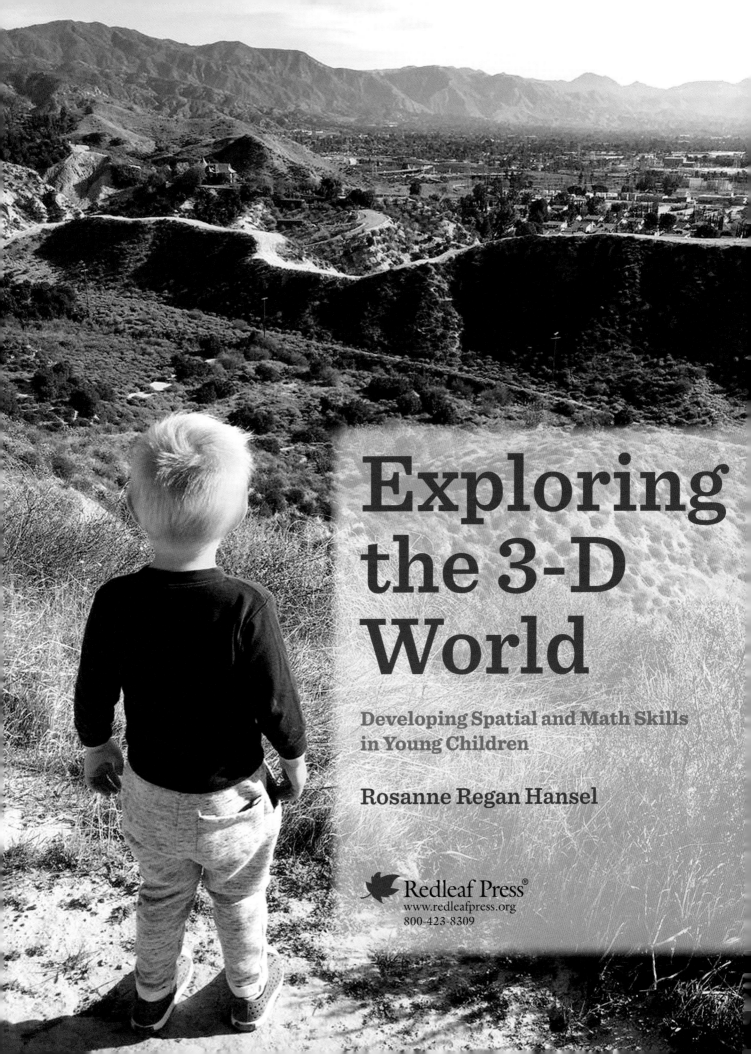

Exploring the 3-D World

Developing Spatial and Math Skills in Young Children

Rosanne Regan Hansel

Redleaf Press®
www.redleafpress.org
800-423-8309

Published by Redleaf Press
10 Yorkton Court
St. Paul, MN 55117
www.redleafpress.org

First edition 2021
Cover design by Renee Hammes
Cover photographs by Jacie Engel, Kathleen Spadola Whalen, and Kate Rosander
Interior layout by Wendy Holdman
Typeset in Sentinel
Interior photos by Kelly Bhatia, Pam Bonsell, Jennifer Campanile, Kristen Cecchini, Kim Ciemniecki, Krista Crumrine, Columba Del Pizzo, Emily Engel, Efekan Ersoy, Yetkin Etkin, Rosanne Hansel, Amber Jarrett, Sean Kelly, Filma Marchishin, Lisa Pangborn, Kate Rosander, Madison Savulich, Laura Smoot, Kate Szczubelek, Heather Terantino, Suzanne Toriello, Kathleen Spadola Whalen, and Carolyn Wiley
Printed in the United States of America
28 27 26 25 24 23 22 21   1 2 3 4 5 6 7 8

Library of Congress Cataloging-in-Publication Data

Names: Hansel, Rosanne Regan, author.
Title: Exploring the 3-D world : developing spatial and math skills in young children / by Rosanne Regan Hansel.
Description: First edition. | St. Paul, MN : Redleaf Press, 2021. | Includes bibliographical references and index.
    | Summary: "We live in a 3-D world, but many of our learning environments today offer few opportunities
    for three-dimensional exploration. Spatial reasoning is also integral to everyday life, in social studies, the
    arts, and geography as well as new careers like computer animation. *Exploring the 3-D World* will help early
    childhood teachers feel confident in implementing more mathematical and spatial concepts into their rooms"—
    Provided by publisher.
Identifiers: LCCN 2020049131 (print) | LCCN 2020049132 (ebook) | ISBN 9781605546926 (paperback : alk. paper) |
    ISBN 9781605546933 (ebook)
Subjects: LCSH: Mathematics—Study and teaching (Early childhood) | Spatial ability in children.
Classification: LCC QA135.6 .H364 2021 (print) | LCC QA135.6 (ebook) | DDC 372.7—dc23
LC record available at https://lccn.loc.gov/2020049131
LC ebook record available at https://lccn.loc.gov/2020049132

Printed on acid-free paper

This book is dedicated, with love, to Dagan and Aspen.

With you on the West Coast and me on the East Coast, the space between us is too wide!

Using my new dimension-shifting skills, I will take giant steps from here to there

to give you big hugs and kisses!

Contents

Foreword

If you were to ask teachers to talk about the importance of spatial thinking, many of them would not be able to express its significance or give examples of it. Teachers often cannot see spatial development's connections in their daily lives, especially because spatial development has often been overlooked in favor of the emphasis on literacy and number sense in our schools. Nonetheless, it is particularly important for STEM (Science, Technology, Engineering, and Math) as well as the arts.

Rosanne has elevated the often-unobserved skill of spatial development in early childhood to a new prominence that teachers will observe and significantly value in their early childhood programs, and she has greatly extended the possibilities for the important skill of spatial literacy for the reader. She has used research from cognitive researchers and the STEM fields to make the case that spatial learning is crucial for young children. The connections to spatial development need to be made at school, home, libraries, and museums while children are playing, and Rosanne does this at a multifaceted level. She has managed to capture and pass on to her readers examples of a variety of unique spatial skills demonstrated by children in different settings.

Many people think that spatial ability is innate, but it can be learned, and it can be an integral part of a play-based curriculum. Teachers and parents, however, need to support spatial understandings with skillful guidance, and Rosanne has shown through a myriad of examples how to promote these concepts. She offers many open-ended activities as well as guided activities to promote spatial development. She encourages teachers to pay close attention to spatial skills and understand that these skills are an entryway to math skills such as subitizing and recognizing two- and three-dimensional shapes.

This book echoes and extends the work of historical figures who emphasized block building, including Friedrich Fröbel and Patty Smith Hill. However, Rosanne has taken the concepts in spatial development to a higher, more comprehensive level with two- and three-dimensional objects. Rosanne's art and early childhood background have enhanced her many ideas with geometric shapes and patterns and her unique ideas for transforming, composing, and decomposing figures. The inclusive examples bear witness to little architects and engineers becoming creative spatial thinkers. Building is an important part of play, the initial step in a child's education. Play can encompass manipulating objects at a basic level, but in extended play children can tackle complex construction and artistic problems. This helps children grow into adults who are problem solvers.

Exploring the 3-D World will turn spatial development from an overlooked skill to a focused skill for all teachers to promote throughout their classrooms. This book will benefit so many organizations interested in promoting the STEM arts through the interdisciplinary use of spatial development. Expanding on her previous award-winning book, *Creative Block Play*, Rosanne's work will increase the value and significance we place on spatial problem solving in our early childhood programs.

—Mary Jo Pollman, PhD
Professor Emerita, Early Childhood Education
Metropolitan State University, Denver, Colorado
Author of *Blocks and Beyond: Strengthening Early Math and Science Skills through Spatial Learning* and *The Young Artist as Scientist: What Can Leonardo Teach Us?*

Acknowledgments

This book would not have been possible without the contributions of extremely dedicated early childhood educators and administrators from several New Jersey school districts. They went above and beyond sharing inspiring stories and photos of the children you see featured in this book. I extend my deepest appreciation to Kate Rosander, elementary supervisor at Scotch Plains–Fanwood Regional School District, for her expert feedback and for supporting her teachers over the years in documenting their students' progress in spatial learning. My heartfelt thanks go out to the following preschool and kindergarten teachers from Scotch Plains–Fanwood: Jennifer Campanile, Kristen Cecchini, Kim Ciemniecki, Karen Glod, Filma Marchishin, Madison Savulich, Laura Smoot, Kate Szczubelek, Heather Terantino, Suzanne Toriello, and especially Amber Jarrett and Kelly Bhatia, who so graciously invited me into their classrooms. I thank Katie Spadola Whalen for her inspiring guidance to these teachers at Scotch Plains–Fanwood and for photo contributions from her classroom and home setting. Warmest thanks to Dr. Jorie Quinn, STEM specialist, and kindergarten teacher Krista Crumrine from the Union City School District, for their continuing enthusiasm and contributions. Many thanks to former director of early childhood Dr. Renee Whelan (now assistant professor at William Paterson University) and math supervisor Melanie Harding at Long Branch Public Schools, who invited me to speak about spatial development. First-grade teachers Kevin Gilbert, Lisa Pangborn, and Tracey Cummings and kindergarten teachers Sean Kelly and Michelle Fiore deserve a big thanks for their photos. Heartfelt thanks to James DeSimone, curriculum supervisor of early childhood education at the Mount Laurel Schools, and Carolyn Wiley, kindergarten teacher at Parkway Elementary School. I so appreciate the invitation to visit the Mountain Villa School in Allamuchy Township School District and the contributions of kindergarten teachers Catherine Cefaloni, Robin Samiljan, and Paige Schmiedeke and their administrator, Melissa Sobel.

At the 2019 conference of the National Association for the Education of Young Children (NAEYC), I attended the inspiring session "Building Developmentally Appropriate Learning Environments for Spatial Thinking: Understanding Learning Trajectories for Maps and Coordinates," presented by Dr. Kevser Koc, PhD, associate professor in early childhood education at Istanbul Medeniyet University, and Dr. Yusuf Koc, PhD, associate professor of mathematics education at Kocaeli

University (Koc and Koc 2019). Each agreed to share photos and stories from the Çam Koleji school located in the Kartal district of Istanbul, Turkey. My sincerest thanks to the teachers at Çam Koleji, Nergis Sunbul Dogan, Seher Eksi, Yasemin Yildirim, Dr. Kevser Koc, and Dr. Yusuf Koc, for taking the time to contribute examples of what young children can do when given adult guidance. A special note of appreciation to school founder Mr. Nevzat Çam and the school governing board for supporting this research and work.

I was fascinated to hear Dr. Doug Clements present "Children's Mathematical Thinking, B-Grade 3: Using the Learning and Teaching Trajectories Tool to Teach Arithmetic" at the same NAEYC conference. I have included in this book only a tiny fraction of the incredible work that he and Dr. Julie Sarama have contributed to early childhood education. I so appreciate Dr. Clements's answers to my many questions following his presentation and hope you will visit www.learning trajectories.org for more information.

The Boulder Journey School in Boulder, Colorado, is known for its innovative programs for young children. Alison Maher, executive director; Andrea Sisbarro and Vicki Oleson, school directors; Alex Cruickshank Morgan, community outreach specialist; and Jacie Engel, studio specialist, shared their extraordinary visual documentation of "The Exploring Boulder Game." They were also gracious enough to provide photos from their "Digital Humanities" presentation at the 2019 NAEYC conference, which gives the early childhood field new perspectives on the "T" aspect of STEM. I cannot thank the Boulder Journey School enough for permission to use their outstanding photos and stories.

Inspired at a workshop on block play by kindergarten teacher Kathleen Blass and preschool teacher Carrie Williams, I accepted an invitation from director Laura Sacco to visit the Charlestown Playhouse in Phoenixville, Pennsylvania. It was amazing to see well-loved blocks that were more than eighty years old still at the center of the curriculum. Many thanks to all the teachers who so warmly welcomed me to their classrooms, especially Kathleen Blass, Carrie Williams, Cindy Shillinger, and Rachel Applegate.

Beyond the early childhood classroom, we applaud the parents and grandparents who support spatial development by offering their little ones opportunities to explore the three-dimensional world. I am forever grateful to Pam Bonsell, Cecilia Tubo, Katie Whalen, and Emily and Jeffrey Engel for sharing their photos!

My eternal thanks to all the participants in the hundreds of workshops and seminars I have facilitated over the years. I continue to be inspired by your willingness, despite the overwhelming demands on you, to step out of your comfort zones to try out new ideas and strategies. I've included a few of the creative constructions and amazing drawings from the 2019 workshops.

I extend my profound appreciation to all the researchers, educators, and writers who have blazed new territory in bringing spatial development to the attention of those who care for and teach young children. The 2017 article in *EdWeek* by Jill Berkowicz and Ann Myers was the impetus I needed to set the ball in motion for this book, which was first sparked by the new research on spatial development I had discovered for my book *Creative Block Play*. In addition to Mary Jo Pollman, Douglas Clements, and Julie Sarama, in this book you will see names such as Kelly Fisher, Brian Verdine, Kathy Hirsh-Pasek, Nora Newcombe, Roberta Golinkoff, Susan Golbeck, Elizabeth Gunderson, Susan Levine, Brenna Hassinger-Das, David Lubinski, Sheryl Sorby, David Uttal, Jonathan Wai, and so many others who have inspired my thinking about spatial learning. You will also see many references to Ontario's Ministry of Education and Joan Moss, Catherine Bruce, Bev Caswell, Tara Flynn, Zachary Hawes, and the K–2 educators who have done an incredible job of documenting their work on spatial thinking in Toronto, Canada. Thank you Jo Boaler and Deborah Stipek for reminding us that everyone can learn mathematics, and to Karen Worth, Ingrid Chalufour, and Jeffrey Winokur for guiding me when I was the early childhood specialist for the National Science Foundation–funded Math Science Partnership at Rutgers University and for helping me understand the science of inquiry and the importance of representation.

From my beginnings as an art educator, I have been astounded by the many connections between the arts and STEM. I am thankful to Cathy Weisman Topal for her contributions to both these worlds and for introducing me to the process of line printing. It was also Cathy who urged me to read Mary Jo Pollman's book *Blocks and Beyond: Strengthening Math and Science Skills through Spatial Learning.* Dr. Pollman has written beautifully about these intersections in her books, widening my understanding of both worlds and providing feedback on the first manuscript. I am deeply indebted to her for agreeing to write the foreword to this book.

Many thanks to my agent, MaryAnn Kohl; my editor, Melissa York; art director Renee Hammes; copy editor Christine Florie; Wendy Holdman, layout; Douglas Schmitz, managing editor; marketing and publicity coordinator Meredith Burks; and the entire production staff at Redleaf for working out all the kinks along the way and for transforming a 2-D manuscript into a visually engaging 3-D book on math and spatial development.

My love and gratitude to colleagues and friends Pam Brillante, Karen Nemeth, Barbara Tkach, and Elizabeth Vaughan for their vital contributions to the early childhood world, for keeping me abreast of important early childhood topics I might otherwise have overlooked, and for their most-appreciated ongoing support and encouragement.

It is easy to get carried away with an idea about how we can do a better job of helping young children develop spatial skills and thus give everyone an equal shot at achieving their highest potential. Reading Ann Pelo and Margie Carter's book *From Teaching to Thinking* and Erika Christakis's book *The Importance of Being Little* while in the process of writing this book reminded me that nothing is as important as the caring relationship between adult and child in the learning process. And while I have always believed in play-based learning, the new research on guided play cited in this book underscores that point and urges us to become even more attentive to mastering the art of teaching. May we never forget this!

My humblest thanks and deepest appreciation go to all the remarkable children who appear in this book and made amazing contributions. Finally, to my family—David, Amber, Andy, Jennifer, Emily, and Jeff—for their continuing love and support. I have dedicated this book to my beloved grandchildren Dagan and Aspen, who fill my life with incredible joy and give me so much hope for the future.

Introduction

We live in a 3-D world, but many of our learning environments offer few opportunities for three-dimensional exploration. A wide variety of hands-on tools are available that are known to improve cognitive development, yet we invest millions of dollars in curriculum materials that are inappropriate for young children. Our world is one of images, but our classrooms are frequently geared toward teaching words and numbers. Ironically, new brain research and child development studies are filling professional journals with mounting evidence that early childhood educators, those who care for and teach children from birth to age eight, need to start paying greater attention to spatial skill development. Exploring the 3-D world is key to building spatial skills in the early years. However, interacting with two- and three-dimensional materials, and learning to use and interpret images along with words and numbers, are also crucial aspects of spatial development.

As an educator who taught the visual arts to elementary-age schoolchildren, I was convinced that the spatial and perceptual experiences they had during art explorations benefited them in ways not typically acknowledged in the education world. For example, during an exploration of architecture, preschool and kindergarten children learn about geometric shapes, both 2-D (rectangle-shaped windows and doors or triangle-shaped roofs) and 3-D (cylinder-shaped towers and cone-shaped steeples) in the built environment. Positioning themselves in front of or beside a building, children observe building exteriors from many different perspectives and then draw what they see. They learn about builders' blueprints and how to create floor plans, imagining themselves with a bird's-eye view of a familiar room or making maps as they plan out a city. Through trial and error children learn about scale when they calculate how many cars fit into a garage made out of magnetic tiles or how big to make an enclosure of blocks so three children can fit inside. These authentic play-based explorations are prime opportunities for learning spatial skills in the early years.

In her presentation "Architecture and the Hundred Languages of Children," Ann Gadzikowski (2019) wondered why the study of architecture isn't more prevalent in early childhood curricula. The children's books Gadzikowski featured in her workshop as a provocation for playful explorations focus on architecture and literature and are a perfect accompaniment to the construction materials found in most early childhood classrooms. They are also an excellent way to introduce and teach spatial skills. I have included a few of her suggestions, in addition to my own, in the chapters that follow.

We know that spatial skills are far more important to achievement than previously realized (McClure et al. 2017). Having good spatial skills strongly predicts a child's future achievement in science, technology, engineering, and math (STEM) subjects (Lubinski 2013; Uttal et al. 2013) and mathematics in particular (Clements 2019). For example, scientists say that there is a relationship between playing with puzzles and blocks, having a strong number sense, and being able to solve computation problems (Moss et al. 2016). Because of this growing body of research, the National Council of Teachers of Mathematics (NCTM) has recommended that a stronger focus be placed on spatial reasoning in pre-K–eighth-grade math education (Schwartz 2017). If we truly want to close the achievement gap, researchers say that we must start in the early years. Children living in poverty, children with disabilities, English-language learners, and any child who learns better with a visual-spatial approach to STEM subjects will benefit from the development of their spatial skills. Chapter 1 will provide a definition of spatial skills and why they are important.

While we know that spatial reasoning skills are critical to STEM subjects and provide equitable access for underrepresented populations, helping children excel in math and be prepared for STEM careers is not our only goal. There is much we can do to help children navigate and understand the world around them, cultivating their curiosity, persistence, and intellectual capacity beyond the narrow definitions of academic achievement. After visiting the extraordinary early childhood centers in Reggio Emilia, Italy, Reggio-inspired schools in the United States, and the preschools of Auckland, New Zealand, where abundant resources are available for creating the highest quality learning environments for young children, it is painfully apparent that we could be doing more for young children, especially those living in poverty, throughout the United States. Pelo and Carter echo this sentiment when they state that "poverty definitely has an impact on the child and family, but so do rich experiences, provocative and engaging environments and quality interactions" (2018, 344). All too often play has been eliminated for these children and replaced with paper and pencil activities in order to meet a long list of learning goals and standards. You are sure to be inspired by the teachers you will meet in this book who have not forgotten the importance of what Pelo and Carter call "intellectually rigorous, full-hearted teaching" (2018, 29) as they playfully integrate the spatial skills needed for STEM success and for all areas of life.

What can we do to infuse spatial skills into the curriculum and everyday life? A wealth of information is now available from research to guide best practices that support spatial learning. Chapter 2 summarizes many of the strategies for teaching math and spatial skills recommended in this literature, starting with the basic fact that it is critically important for teachers to understand what spatial skills are. Here I recommend joining professional learning communities, communities of practice, and other models that encourage practitioners to meet in order to connect theory to practice. One example would be to meet with interested colleagues on a regular basis, using this book as a guide to plan spatial activities and to inspire reflection and discussion as you implement these playful explorations in your classroom.

Many experts find that children benefit from regularly engaging in a variety of tasks across subjects, guided by their interests and responses, rather than through discrete lessons squeezed into an already crowded curriculum. For example, children can learn important spatial skills, such as composing, decomposing, turning, and rotating, while playing with blocks. Having time to engage in play with a variety of materials is critically important to fostering spatial skills, but we know that is not enough. The experts say that children are unlikely to learn the intended concept solely through play (Seo and Ginsburg in Moss et al. 2016; Verdine et al. 2017) but rather require adult guidance to maximize understanding. Chapter 3 introduces the idea of "guided play," where adults offer feedback to scaffold children's learning. During guided play children are provided materials and opportunities for learning that focus on spatial skills while adults guide children to a deeper understanding of those skills and encourage the use of spatial language in context. Chapter 3 goes on to outline the essential components necessary to plan a playful exploration that is focused on spatial skill development.

Based on the research outlined in chapters 1 and 2 and the essential components of a playful exploration in chapter 3, chapters 4 to 9 feature key spatial skills that researchers have identified as important for young children to learn. The skills are accompanied with illustrated examples of activities designed for children ages four to six. These authentic examples come from public preschool and kindergarten classrooms, private preschools and child care centers, and home settings. While the activities in this book are primarily geared for children in preschool and kindergarten, some can be adapted for younger or older children. You will see that each chapter in this book focuses on specific spatial skills, with ideas to support spatial skills in learning centers, a list of important spatial skills and vocabulary, suggested questions and conversation starters to expand learning, ideas for experiential activities to try at home, and recommended children's books that reinforce the spatial skills introduced. In every case the important spatial concepts will be clearly presented so that both children and adults trying out these ideas for the first time can become more skilled at observing, questioning, exploring, and reflecting to deepen understanding of each concept.

In chapter 10 we will take a look at how visual representations, such as documentation of children's experiences and displays of data in graphs and charts, are helpful in opening new pathways to learning across the curriculum. Also covered is how visual representations, such as drawing, can be an important tool in the development of spatial skills.

It is not the intention of this book to prescribe activities to be copied step-by-step. Once you have a better understanding of spatial skills, I hope you will be inspired by the teachers and children featured on these pages to challenge yourself and your students to create your own spatial learning experiences based on newly discovered passions and interests.

Embracing the importance of spatial skills and starting to incorporate more playful explorations into your classroom may seem overwhelming. However, remember that children are phenomenal learners, full of curiosity and joy. When you share in their excitement in learning while guiding the children to deeper understanding, you will be amazed and inspired by what very young children can accomplish!

Part One

What We Know about Teaching Spatial Skills

Definition and Rationale for Teaching Spatial Skills in the Early Years

Because you are reading this book, you may already be convinced that you should be teaching spatial skills in your early childhood classroom. I have found, however, that most teachers have little guidance from their curriculum materials on what spatial skills are, why it is so important to support children in developing these critical skills, what type of activities strengthen spatial skills, and what strategies they can use to support spatial learning.

DEFINING SPATIAL THINKING

Spatial skills have been studied for more than a hundred years, but the definition of spatial skills varies depending on the field—be it geography, cognitive psychology, art, science, mathematics, or engineering (Sorby 1999). It can be confusing! In this book we will use the definition provided by the US National Research Council in its publication *Learning to Think Spatially*: "Spatial reasoning, or thinking, involves the location and movement of objects and ourselves, either mentally or physically in space" (National Research Council in Ontario Ministry of Education 2014, 3). We will focus primarily on spatial skills in STEM with an emphasis on mathematics, using the general term "spatial skills."

A think tank of mathematicians, math educators, and psychologists from Canada, Australia, and the United States has developed a list of actions included in spatial thinking skills, including perspective taking, visualizing, locating, orienting, dimension shifting, pathfinding, sliding, rotating, reflecting, diagramming, modeling, symmetrizing, composing, decomposing, scaling, mapmaking, and designing (Davis, Okamoto, and Whitely in Moss et al. 2016; Ontario Ministry 2014). This list provides the organizing framework for playful explorations promoting spatial skills that you will find in part 2. Note that each of these spatial skills does not fit neatly into a chapter heading, and many of the explorations introduced in one category can actually nurture more than one spatial thinking skill.

Research shows that there are seven basic reasons why we should be helping children develop spatial thinking skills in the early years.

1. Spatial skills are essential for functioning in our day-to-day world

Having good spatial sense helps us pack our luggage, select the appropriate-sized container for storing leftovers, and follow a map so we don't get lost. In her article on improving spatial skills in children, Dr. Gwen Dewar defines it beautifully when she says, "It's the mental feat that architects and engineers perform when they design buildings. The capacity that permits a chemist to contemplate the structure of a molecule, or a surgeon to navigate the human body. It's what Michelangelo used when he visualized a future sculpture trapped inside a lump of stone" (2018). When you really think about it, and as you learn more about spatial orientation in chapter 9, there are many fields beyond STEM that require strong spatial thinking skills, such as architecture, the arts, geography, professional sports (Ontario Ministry 2014), and many others that we haven't even dreamed of yet.

2. Spatial thinking is important in many subject areas

Knowing that spatial thinking skills are critical in many fields, it only makes sense that spatial thinking is also important in many subject areas in school. For example, spatial knowledge is basic to organizing words on a page from left to right (for the English language) and in understanding how to use horizontal, vertical, and diagonal lines to make the shapes of specific letters (Golbeck 2005). The arts are filled with opportunities that engage spatial skills, whether through manipulating shapes and forms while working with clay or moving the body through dance or dramatic play. The visual arts, in particular, are most often seen as a means for self-expression in the early years, and while that is extremely important for young children, embedding spatial thinking skills in the visual arts should not be overlooked. We will provide explorations in part 2 that you can try in your early childhood classroom or at home.

In *Learning to Think Spatially*, the National Research Council issued a call to educators "to recognize spatial thinking as important not only across mathematical strands but also across subject areas" by infusing spatial thinking into existing curricular objectives (National Research Council in Ontario Ministry 2014, 5). For early childhood educators, integrating spatial learning in all areas of the curriculum is just as important as addressing the physical, social-emotional, and cognitive development of the whole child.

3. Spatial thinking plays a critical role in learning mathematics

Research findings from psychology and neuroscience as well as education are converging to highlight the importance of spatial skills. According to one study (Gunderson et al. 2012), for example, over the course of one school year, children's spatial skills in first and second grade predicted improvements in linear number line knowledge. This may come as a surprise to many early childhood educators and even some math specialists who have focused solely on numeracy in the early years, but research has shown that "children will not learn number and operations, which includes solving problems involving these topics, unless they also learn spatial reasoning" (Clements in Moss et al. 2016). Susan Levine, a leading authority on spatial and mathematical learning, adds that improving children's spatial thinking at a young age not only may help foster skills specific to spatial reasoning, but also improves symbolic numerical representations (Gunderson et al. 2012).

In 1967 Jean Piaget came to the conclusion that young children didn't learn mathematics through verbal instruction alone but rather through hands-on interaction with many kinds of materials (Hirsch 1996). However, we are now just beginning to understand the interplay between spatial reasoning (especially with manipulatives such as blocks and puzzles) and mathematics. We know that by focusing on spatial thinking, we can tap into a child's diverse strengths. New research on spatial thinking underscores the importance of spatial reasoning skills in geometry, measurement, and problem solving in children's early math experiences (Shumway in Ontario Ministry 2014). Because of this growing body of research, the NCTM has recommended that a stronger focus be placed on spatial reasoning in pre-K–eighth-grade math education (Schwartz 2017).

4. Spatial thinking is a predictor of achievement in STEM careers

When children are just learning to speak, write, and count, teachers and parents are probably not thinking about preparing them for career paths, even though we know that good spatial skills strongly predict achievement and attainment in STEM fields (Uttal, Miller, and Newcombe in Berkowicz and Myers 2017). You may ask, why worry about spatial skills while children are so young? One reason to start early is because it is becoming increasingly clear from the research that strengthening executive function skills, such as working memory and attention along with early spatial skills, improves children's math scores (Verdine et al. in Berkowicz and Myers 2017). And when you consider that young children who may not be exceptional in mathematical or verbal abilities might have strong, but overlooked, spatial abilities, we are leaving an untapped pool of talent for STEM careers (Wai, Lubinski, and Benbow 2009).

5. Spatial thinking is an overlooked area of STEM instruction

When the insightful report *STEM Starts Early: Grounding Science, Technology, Engineering, and Math Education in Early Childhood* (McClure et al. 2017) first appeared, it brought attention to the barriers that exist in supporting early STEM learning. Some of those barriers include the need for additional STEM training for teachers so that they can engage young children in developmentally appropriate STEM learning; the need for more connections between school, home, and community learning environments, such as libraries and museums; and the lack of research and policy to support STEM learning in the early years. However, citing important research on spatial development, authors Berkowicz and Myers (2017) argue that spatial skills were overlooked as a key feature of STEM education in the report. Echoing this concern, mathematics educators and researchers in Toronto, Canada (Moss et al. 2016), also noticed a curious neglect of spatial reasoning in their math curriculum and took action to create one, Math 4 Young Children, that included spatial-focused activities.

If we know that improving children's spatial skills has a positive impact on their future success in STEM disciplines, then we need to incorporate spatial skills more explicitly and recognize the critical role they play in children's development. As Berkowicz and Myers state, "We must increase awareness of what spatial skills involve, their relevance to everyday life and STEM success, and how we can support young children's spatial development as part of our improvements in STEM education" (2017, 3).

6. Spatial thinking provides equitable access to math for all children

Despite efforts to close the math achievement gap for children from communities with low socioeconomic status where children of color disproportionately reside, the gap remains throughout elementary, middle, and high school (National Assessment of Educational Progress in Davis and Farran 2019). Improving access to quality math instruction is a matter of social justice. Knowing the connection between spatial thinking and success in math, there is much work to be done to include spatial skills with instruction and intervention (Jordan and Levine in Ontario Ministry 2014, 9).

Identifying children's spatial abilities, which often go unrecognized, and using those strengths to learn math is an important step in reaching underserved populations. In addition to children from underresourced communities, this includes girls and children with learning disabilities, particularly difficulties in learning math. Assessments to measure spatial ability have been around for decades, but since they don't cover the full range of spatial skills and aren't typically designed for young children, this book recommends performance-based assessments as introduced in chapter 2 and outlined in chapter 3 as one way to identify and strengthen spatial skills.

While not specifically focused on spatial thinking skills, the team of STEM experts called together by the US Department of Education (2016) Office of Innovation and Improvement put forth an urgent call for early exposure to and engagement in STEM learning experiences, as well as equitable access, in its report *STEM 2026*.

7. Spatial thinking can be improved

For many years people believed that spatial ability was something you either had or you didn't. In 2013 a team of researchers led by David Uttal summarized two decades of research on spatial training. They concluded that all age groups can improve spatial thinking with practice, through familiar activities such as puzzle play, block building, and art and design tasks (Uttal et al. 2013).

The bottom line is that intentionally designed, play-based spatial explorations with adult guidance can improve math and spatial skills for all children. The next chapter will provide an overview of what the research tells us about successful strategies for teaching these critical math and spatial skills.

Strategies for Teaching Math and Spatial Skills

As discussed in chapter 1, spatial skills are important and can be improved through early education and experience. In early childhood education, we understand that teaching discrete spatial skills is not as effective as integrating them across all areas of a play-based curriculum. The teaching strategies shared below are from the leading experts in mathematics and spatial skill development.

KNOW WHAT SPATIAL SKILLS ARE AND OVERCOME ANXIETIES ABOUT TEACHING THEM

Knowledge of what spatial skills are and how best to support spatial development in children is evolving. The definition and justification for teaching spatial skills proposed here is just the beginning. Keeping up to date with new research through readings and professional development increases teachers' familiarity and comfort with teaching spatial skills. Participating in workshops where there are opportunities for hands-on exploration with three-dimensional materials, as illustrated in the photos below, helps build new perspectives in introducing these skills in the classroom.

Workshops are a good place to start, but having support during the initial phase of implementation helps teachers gain confidence in teaching spatial skills and strengthens their instruction. In the Scotch Plains–Fanwood Regional School District in New Jersey, elementary education supervisor Kate Rosander created a community of practice for preschool and kindergarten teachers offering professional development on specific spatial reasoning skills and facilitating discussions on best practices in teaching them. You will see examples throughout this book showcasing the successes and challenges teachers experienced as they documented their work with children. Here is Kate's story:

> **Mrs. Kate Rosander, Elementary Education Supervisor,**
> **Scotch Plains–Fanwood Regional School District, New Jersey**
>
> *"What began as a simple invitation to contribute photographs to this book quickly blossomed into a collaborative journey of inquiry alongside fourteen dedicated preschool and kindergarten teachers. Over the course of several months, we read research, observed children, shared stories, and asked questions to better understand how children develop spatial reasoning and what role we, as educators, played in that development. The photographs of children in action became a springboard for reflection, which started with our noticing what children were doing and led to wonderings of 'why' and 'what if.' Why did boys frequent the block center more often than girls? What would happen if we introduced smaller blocks, added accessories, provided authentic examples, or changed the classroom space so that more children could build simultaneously? Why did children struggle with creating radial patterns when line printing? What would happen if we encouraged them to rotate their papers while working? These questions piqued our curiosities, challenged our thinking, and ultimately opened doors to improving our practice to best meet the needs of our youngest learners."*

UNDERSTAND WHAT TYPES OF ACTIVITIES SUPPORT SPATIAL DEVELOPMENT

An experienced early childhood teacher knows that standards and curricula should guide, not dictate, instruction because each child requires us to make adjustments in our approach to meet their needs. This is even truer when guiding children in developing spatial skills. Because spatial skills are rarely addressed in most curricula, it is necessary to target specific spatial skills by supplementing the curriculum (Stipek 2019).

Understanding that teachers are already overwhelmed by the demands of a crowded curriculum, Newcombe (2013) suggests "spatializing" the existing curriculum by infusing spatial skills into the school day. She says you can easily incorporate puzzles, promote guided play with blocks and geometric shapes, read books with spatial words in them, include spatial skills in the visual arts, and encourage spatial learning both inside and outside the classroom. This is a great place to start, but we know that it is not enough. Teachers need support as they plan and implement these activities.

In a university setting in Istanbul, Turkey, Professors Kevser Koc and Yusuf Koc partnered to collaborate with kindergarten teachers to develop activities that foster mathematical and spatial reasoning skills. This is their story:

Dr. Kevser Koc, PhD, Associate Professor in Early Childhood Education, Istanbul Medeniyet University, and Dr. Yusuf Koc, PhD, Associate Professor in Mathematics Education, Kocaeli University, Turkey

"We are working with kindergarten children at a private school, Çam Schools in Kartal, [a district in] Istanbul, Turkey. The school houses a middle school, an elementary school, and a kindergarten. The kindergarten has two rooms with mixed-aged children. In each room, there is a master teacher. There is also an assistant teacher working with both master teachers.

"We have been collaborating with these teachers about a year; working through developing and implementing activities to support mathematical and spatial reasoning skills. These activities are based on Learning Trajectories by Clements and Sarama (2014). We used the trajectories as a guide to plan the activities that are developmentally appropriate and challenging enough to provoke children's thinking toward a higher level. Also, we considered children's individual needs and differentiate our instruction.

"Throughout this project, Dr. Kevser Koc visited the school at least once a week and worked with teachers and students to build a richer environment that facilitates children's understanding of spatial orientation. We began with initial basic ideas such as directional, locational, and relational concepts, including 'in,' 'on,' 'under,' 'up' and 'down.' Then, we developed more complex tasks, each time directing children toward more abstract forms of thinking and introducing different representations of space. Children worked in multiple organizations; individual, small groups, and whole class. After about four months, children did not only love those activities, but they also improved a lot. We believe this is just a beginning!"

ORGANIZE THE LEARNING ENVIRONMENT TO PROVIDE MATERIALS AND OPPORTUNITIES TO INVESTIGATE SPATIAL SKILLS

Providing diagrams, maps, graphs, drawings, photographs, and visual daily schedules is important to creating a rich learning environment (Ontario Ministry 2014). Children require different methods, pathways, and representations for learning math (Boaler 2016) and for applying spatial skills to all other subject areas (more on this in chapter 10).

In early childhood classroom learning centers, children can be offered meaningful opportunities to investigate mathematical and spatial thinking concepts. By using hands-on materials in the block area, in the math center, or embedded in art, games, and dramatic play, children can broaden their math and spatial skills. Although a few recommendations for technology use are included in this book, research does not show that it is more effective than interactions with real objects (Zosh et al. in Berkowicz and Myers 2017).

Blocks are an excellent example of a 3-D material that helps young children move between concrete representations and abstract ideas, building a deeper understanding of math and spatial concepts.

Block Activities That Support Spatial Skills

Block Activity	Spatial Skill
Constructing with blocks	Transforming shapes by rotating, sliding, or flipping them (making as many combinations as possible through manipulation)
Filling containers with blocks; filling enclosures with objects	Learning to judge capacity and volume. How many can fit in the container? Does the object fit in the enclosure?
Fitting blocks together and taking them apart	Decomposing (part-whole integration that involves seeing the shapes embedded in other shapes and seeing them as a whole)
Changing the shape and arrangements of blocks by stacking or enclosing them	Composing (physically or mentally combining shapes to make different shapes)
Observing block constructions from different viewpoints, such as from above, from behind, or in front of a mirror	Perspective taking (considering the perspective of someone who is in a different location and how that view might be different from yours)
Describing positions, directions, and distances, such as outside, inside, over, and under, while building	Using spatial language in context while building

Continued on next page.

Block Activities That Support Spatial Skills (continued)

Block Activity	Spatial Skill
Building on the floor or outdoors	Knowing your body's position and where it is in space (spatial awareness, spatial orientation)
Using blocks to represent other objects	Representing symbolically one object for another
Interpreting spatial relations in drawings, pictures, and photos	Using nonverbal reasoning; seeing connections between 3-D objects and 2-D representations
Drawing 3-D constructions or reproducing real-life structures	Understanding spatial relationships and reinforcing visual-spatial memory
Comparing and measuring the size, shape, thickness, length, and height of blocks	Comparing objects; scaling up or down (imagining objects or amounts as proportionally larger or smaller)
Making a model from a map or blueprint	Visually interpreting maps and blueprints
Building a bridge	Learning to judge the distance between objects; learning to fit blocks together and balance them
Designing with blocks	Creating patterns (radial, linear, symmetrical, tessellations)
Playing hide-and-seek with blocks	Locating and remembering locations of objects
Putting blocks back on the shelves (marked with the shape of the blocks)	Classifying, sorting, and sequencing shapes

MAKE MATH LEARNING EXPERIENCES CHALLENGING, COLLABORATIVE, AND PLAYFUL

A rich learning environment with hands-on materials for exploring is important, but it is not enough if we want children to develop strong spatial skills. Stanford professor Dr. Deborah Stipek, who studies early childhood math and motivation, says that children do not learn solely through play (2017). When thinking specifically about spatial skills, the teachers who contributed to this book found this to be true. Spatial concepts and vocabulary typically did not surface in children's play but had to be intentionally planned with clear learning goals, appropriate materials, and skillful guidance.

Learning math doesn't have to be painful, however. Stipek insists that "young children enjoy learning math and can learn far more than was previously assumed—without a single flashcard or worksheet" (2019, 59). Dr. Jo Boaler, a Stanford mathematics educator and author of *Mathematical Mindsets*, agrees that the traditional methods used in math education don't work. She is convinced that we kill curiosity and creativity when we expect children to work alone on meaningless worksheets instead of allowing them to work collaboratively to solve a problem they care about (Boaler 2016).

Piaget said that learning is the "mindful construction of new knowledge based on hypothesis testing and revising one's own knowledge," but he emphasized that a hallmark of this type of inquiry-based education was learning through play (Zosh et al. 2018, 3). One of the challenges identified by STEM experts who authored the *STEM 2026* report (US Department of Education 2016) was the need to redesign learning activities to be more play-based and less centered on a prescribed set of activities. Chapter 3 will show how it is possible to promote spatial thinking skills in challenging, collaborative, and playful explorations.

EMPHASIZE SPATIAL LANGUAGE, SPATIAL THINKING, AND THE USE OF GESTURES THROUGHOUT THE DAY

Teaching and modeling specific spatial words (such as *left, right, above, below*) throughout the day has been correlated to children's spatial ability. Studies have shown that children who were taught spatial language performed better on spatial tasks than children who were not (Tepylo, Moss, and Hawes in Ontario Ministry 2014). One example of an activity using spatial language to promote children's understanding and use of spatial words is number sudoku. In a traditional sudoku game, players complete a grid so that every row and column and 3 x 3 box contains every digit from 1 to 9 inclusively. In this game adapted for younger children, each child is given a 4 x 4 wooden grid and four sets of square tiles numbered from 1 to 4. The teacher guides children in placing a tile next to another tile, under another tile, or between two tiles, or two tiles under another tile. Players are expected to complete the sudoku, making sure no number is repeated in a row or column. Research also shows that the more children are exposed to spatial language, the more likely they

will use that language themselves, especially in the presence of spatial materials such as building blocks (Ferrara et al. in Moss et al. 2016). Throughout the explorations in this book, we encourage parents and educators to emphasize spatial language, including words that describe shapes, positions, movements, comparisons, height, width, length, distance, and properties of a shape or line.

Spatial Language

Location/position words: on, off, on top of, over, under, in, out, into, out of, top, bottom, above, below, in front of, in back of, behind, beside, by, next to, between, in the middle, same/different side, upside down, right, left, north, south, east, west

Movement words: up, down, forward, backward, around, through, to, from, toward, away from, sideways, across, back and forth

Comparison words: larger, smaller, same, more, less, higher, lower

Spatial words that describe height, width, and length: tall, short, wide, narrow, long

Distance words: near, far, close to, far from, shortest/longest path

Transformation words: turn, flip, slide, reflection, rotation, put together, take apart, fold in half

Spatial words that describe properties of a shape or line: curve, point, angle, line, edge, corner, base, face, parallel

Shape vocabulary: see chapter 4

(Moss et al. 2016; Copley 2000)

Young children are not always able to offer verbal explanations for spatial solutions to a problem, especially those who are dual-language learners and those with language delays. Communicating ideas using hand gestures improves spatial thinking (Newcombe 2010). For example, a child might gesture that they want to build a tall structure by standing on their tippy-toes and stretching their hands up high. The child's teachers can help match the word to the child's gestures. "Yes, you want to make your building tall, even higher than your head." Likewise, teachers can help their students understand ordinal numbers as the children line up in first, second, and third place by using body and finger gestures.

ENCOURAGE ACTIVE, PHYSICAL EXPLORATION OF THE REAL WORLD

The *STEM 2026* report features the Smithsonian Early Enrichment Center (SEEC), an early childhood demonstration school in Washington, DC, for children ages two to five that encourages active exploration outside the classroom. Exploring the museum's collections is the foundation of the center's culturally diverse curriculum. Children learn through personal encounters with museum staff as they practice making observations, testing hypotheses, and discussing ideas (US Department of Education 2016). When the children create their own collection of mittens, shoelaces, or other favored objects, they begin to understand the idea of collections as an important mathematical concept.

You can take advantage of opportunities in your own community and offer activities that encourage spatial thinking. In one kindergarten classroom, children visited a local zoo and used a map provided from the zoo as a reference to draw their own zoo maps.

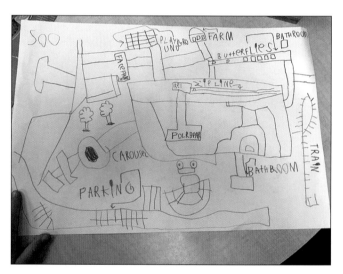

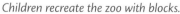
Children recreate the zoo with blocks.

EMPHASIZE THAT SPATIAL SKILLS CAN BE MASTERED WITH SOME TIME AND EFFORT

Many mathematics educators, including Boaler and Stipek, are concerned with the way math is taught. Boaler says we seem to reward those who can come up with the right answer quickly: "Math continues to be presented as a speed race, more than any other subject—timed math tests, flash cards, math apps against the clock. It is no wonder that students who think slowly and deeply are put off by mathematics" (2016, 30). Stipek adds that "strict adherence to pacing guides often results in instruction that is too hard for some children and too easy for others" (2019, 63), taking the focus off the needs of the individual child. The most challenging and important part of teaching is scaffolding, which helps children revisit ideas and learn them deeply.

In chapter 1 we learned that researchers found that spatial skills could be improved with practice. Boaler cites study after study that shows how intelligence can grow, adapt, and change when we have conversations, play games, or build with blocks, to give just a few examples. Yet so many people have been traumatized by math and believe that you are either gifted in math or you aren't. In her work with Carol Dweck, the developer of the idea of growth mindsets, Boaler has found that it is your willingness to persist (growth mindset) that is key to tackling more challenging problems. "If we believe that we can learn, and that mistakes are valuable, our brains grow to a great extent when we make a mistake" (Boaler 2016, 13).

A small percentage of children have disabilities that make math learning difficult, Boaler says, but most (about 95 percent) can learn math. It is important to know that children with poor spatial skills are often slow in making progress at first (Newcombe 2010), so it may take patience on your part to continue reinforcing these critical skills. If spatial activities are age appropriate and playful and adults provide encouragement and support, learning will be less stressful and more enjoyable for children.

Creating a radial pattern, one that starts at a center point with lines or shapes that move outward like the spokes of a wheel, can be challenging for young children. In this story, notice how Daraja is eager and willing to figure it out. As Kate Rosander tells it:

Mrs. Kate Rosander, Elementary Supervisor, Scotch Plains–Fanwood Regional School District, New Jersey

"Moments after being introduced to line printing and radial patterns, Daraja went to task. He worked systematically from the center out, in layers. First, he stamped the circle and put two intersecting lines through it to create the X. Then he added the lines sticking out from the circle one at a time, proceeding around the circle like spokes on a wheel. Next came the lines perpendicular to each spoke to form a T.

"Pausing in thought, Daraja examined his work before adding the next feature, which was the line perpendicular to the top of the T. Again, he worked systematically around the circle, experimenting with the orientation of each line before placing it on the paper. With a quiet excitement and beaming smile, Daraja showcased his finished product."

DEVELOP EQUITABLE APPROACHES FOR REACHING ALL CHILDREN

We learned from the research outlined in chapter 1 that children from low-income communities, predominantly those of color, enter kindergarten with a math achievement gap that persists into high school. We also learned about the need to address gender inequities and to implement new approaches for helping children with learning disabilities, including those with difficulties learning math.

Unfortunately, young children often receive unintended messages about their abilities based on group membership, such as boys being seen as more adept at engineering than girls or children of Asian ancestry being good at math. These messages can influence children's perceptions of themselves and teacher interactions with them (Erikson Institute 2017). In their chapter on fostering positive experiences in the math center, authors Davis and Farran suggest that early childhood teachers can change that perception "by having positive individual interactions, providing opportunities for exploration, extending children's initial interest, and structuring the environment to continuously attract and engage children in math learning," all of which are particularly beneficial for African American boys (Davis and Farran in Masterson and Bohart 2019, 81).

Sheryl Sorby has studied gender differences in spatial abilities (those that are innate) and spatial skills (those that are learned), and although tests of spatial reasoning show that women score lower than men, she is "not interested in arguing why the gap exists because training and practice can close it" (Kris 2016). Sorby believes that regardless of spatial abilities, engaging with spatially rich activities starting at an early age improves spatial skills and sets the stage for later STEM success. This means that teachers and parents must encourage girls to engage in more block and puzzle play, try out engineering and construction toys, make and read maps, and perform other practical spatial tasks. She is a strong advocate of having children build with blocks and then sketch what they constructed, which helps build mental visualization and rotation skills (Sorby 1999).

Children with learning disabilities and difficulties in learning math are another group that specifically require our attention. While we know a great deal about children with difficulties in language development, we don't know as much about identifying and helping children in math. We do know that some children have the learning disability dyscalculia, which means they have trouble understanding and solving math problems as well as learning basic math facts and concepts, such as sorting items by size, shape, and color or repeating simple patterns (Brillante 2017). Some children struggle with subitizing (the ability to know instantly without counting, for example, that five dots on a die is the quantity five), which puts them at serious risk in their mathematical development (Sarama and Clements in Ontario Ministry 2014). Another learning disability related to spatial cognition, spatial acalculia, makes it difficult to read symbols and arrange and write numbers (Mix and Cheng in Ontario Ministry 2014). So that teachers can respond immediately with appropriate activities, accommodations, and guidance, it is critical to have ongoing performance-based assessments that identify learning difficulties.

While not specific to math learning, Universal Design for Learning (UDL) is a scientifically valid framework that provides all students, not just those with disabilities, with multiple ways of acquiring knowledge and skills. According to CAST, the Center for Applied Special Technology (2018), the principles of UDL include providing multiple means of representation, expression, and engagement. For example, help children who are struggling with subitizing by giving them many opportunities to play dice games so they can practice identifying quantity more quickly as they read the die.

Targeting math strategies specifically, Boaler (2016) also emphasizes the importance of having high expectations for all children. In addition, she believes that we need to change opinions about who mathematic achievers are and give girls and children of color additional encouragement and support in this subject. Boaler believes that we can greatly improve math instruction for underserved populations by designing hands-on experiences, project-based learning opportunities, curricula with real-life applications, and opportunities to work together. Paying closer attention to spatial reasoning can provide unexpected entry points into mathematics for all children and improve their prospects for the future and success in later life.

USE AN ONGOING PERFORMANCE-BASED ASSESSMENT TO TRACK PROGRESS ON DEVELOPING SPATIAL SKILLS

Children enter preschool and kindergarten with a wide range of knowledge and skills. For example, Stipek (2019) cites a study that found some children had already mastered most of the math skills in the kindergarten curriculum. She is concerned that in our efforts to support low-achieving children, we should be careful not to overlook high achievers who require challenging mathematical tasks. To support her point, I have witnessed preschool children who can confidently identify and describe 2-D and 3-D shapes spending an inordinate amount of time in kindergarten going over the identification and description of shapes they have already mastered.

Even if spatial skills were included in the tests found in most math curricula, testing preschool and kindergarten-aged children at one point in time is not likely to provide reliable information about their spatial skills. Young children may not be able to demonstrate what they know and can do, for example, if they are anxious to perform in the presence of an unfamiliar examiner, if the test is not given in their home language, or if they are not developmentally ready. In addition, math education specialists like Boaler (2016) believe that testing and grading children discourages them from the important goal of taking on challenges and learning from mistakes in math. And yet if we are not identifying spatial abilities and skills in young children, David Lubinski, a researcher and psychologist at Vanderbilt University, says that "we could be losing some modern-day Edisons and Fords" (Quenqua 2013, 1). For this reason it is important to know where children are in their development of math and spatial skills so that they receive the proper support and reach their highest potential. In its position statement on Early Childhood Curriculum, Assessment and Program Evaluation (2003), the National Association for the Education of Young Children recommends that assessments for children birth through age eight should emphasize observation over time using a performance-based assessment to determine young children's strengths, progress, and needs.

Several of the teachers featured in this book use the birth through grade three performance-based assessment Teaching Strategies GOLD to assess children's understanding of spatial relationships and shapes. For example, kindergarten teachers will observe a child to see if they can "show that shapes remain the same when they are moved, turned, flipped, or slid" and can "break apart [and] combine shapes to create different shapes and sizes" (Teaching Strategies GOLD 2016, 125).

If you are currently not using a performance-based assessment that includes spatial skills, referring to the developmental progressions for spatial thinking outlined by Clements and Sarama (2014) could provide useful information. This research-based framework, called Learning Trajectories, helps teachers guide children on a path to reach specific goals. Preschoolers begin identifying shapes and describing spatial relationships, while kindergartners and children up to grade three begin describing shapes and space; composing and decomposing geometric shapes; judging capacity, length, and height; and describing and analyzing the properties of two-dimensional shapes. Several of the specific goals Clements and Sarama identify for spatial skill development include subitizing, composing 2-D shapes, composing 3-D shapes, spatial orientation, and spatial visualization. For spatial visualization, for instance, they describe developmental levels such as "simple turner," "beginning slider," and "slider, flipper, turner," and provide video examples on their website for each, giving teachers a clearer picture of what children can do (Clements and Sarama 2019).

Understanding the research on teaching mathematics and spatial skills as outlined in this chapter is a major consideration when planning playful explorations and tracking children's progress in acquiring critical spatial skills. Chapter 3 discusses more about how we define play and outlines the essential components of a playful exploration in an early childhood classroom.

Part 2
Playful Explorations

Essential Components of a Playful Exploration

In a high-quality early childhood classroom, learning takes place in the context of play. A solid theoretical base supports the idea that children learn best through play and that, as Erika Christakis puts it, "Play is the fundamental building block of human cognition, emotional health, and social behavior" (2016, 146). But what is play exactly? The truth is there has been a great deal of disagreement about how play should be defined as a mechanism for learning, especially with regard to teaching mathematics. The research on play, along with strategies for teaching math and spatial skills outlined in chapter 2, lays the groundwork for creating explorations that optimize children's spatial skill learning.

OPEN-ENDED FREE PLAY

One definition of play is that it is an activity done for its own sake. Those in early childhood education understand this as the developmentally appropriate practice of valuing process over product and not having a specific goal or outcome in mind. This meaning emphasizes flexibility because children have choices about what they want to do and who they want to do it with. When you observe children in open-ended play, you will see them joyfully engaged. Studies grounded in biological, brain, and educational research substantiate the essential role of free play in healthy child development and as an essential foundation for the skills children will need to live successful lives (American Academy of Pediatrics in Masterson and Bohart 2019).

But do children learn important math concepts in open-ended free play? According to Clements and Sarama (in Moss et al. 2016), research overwhelmingly indicates "that a predominantly free-play approach to mathematics learning is not sufficient to support children from under-resourced communities, and those with learning difficulties, to build the foundational ideas in math that form the pathways to success." Does this mean that most children, especially those considered "at risk" for learning, would benefit primarily from direct instruction? The answer is a resounding no! The research finds that play provides opportunities for "risk taking, confidence building, and the development of self-regulation, metacognition, and logico-mathematical reasoning," all of which are so necessary for deep learning (Bergen in Moss et al. 2016, 24). In addition, play supports the development of dispositions and habits of mind valued in math education, where it is understood that there are many paths to solving a problem (Ginsburg in Moss et al. 2016).

GUIDED PLAY

After many years of rigorous research focused on young children, there is agreement that children do learn from play, but it appears that they can learn so much more with guidance provided by adults (Seo and Ginsburg in Moss et al. 2016, 24). Children's spatial and mathematical skills improve dramatically when they have opportunities to play with spatial toys and games, especially when adults scaffold children's learning in guided play (Verdine et al. 2017). So what is guided play, and how is it different from free play and direct instruction?

In guided play, activities are carefully designed to integrate important learning goals so that the individual child's interests, natural curiosity, social identities, language, culture, and experiences are taken into account (Masterson and Bohart 2019; Moss et al. 2016). The joyful aspects of free play remain while adult feedback and guidance help the child focus on the learning goal (Hassinger-Das, Hirsh-Pasek, and Golinkoff 2019; Zosh et al. 2018). The key is to provide children with the right level of support, or scaffolding, they need to move to the next level of understanding, which requires adults to have a deep connection to and understanding of each child they teach (Christakis 2016).

A study with preschoolers (Fisher et al. 2013) compared children's learning through guided play, free play, and direct instruction. Immediate, targeted feedback from the adult during guided play resulted in children learning more about geometry and shapes than the children who learned in a direct instruction or free play condition. The scaffolding adults provided seemed to prevent frustration and enabled children to engage for longer periods of playful experimentation (Hassinger-Das, Hirsh-Pasek, and Golinkoff 2019). Other experts (Golbeck 2005; Moss et al. 2016) agree that children benefit from regularly engaging in a variety of tasks across subjects as active contributors guided by their interests and responses, rather than through discrete lessons.

New thinking about guided play clarifies some of the confusion about the adult's role in play. Play is described as a spectrum. It can range from free play with no adult guidance or supported play that is more goal oriented with purposeful adult support that still includes child-directed, playful elements (Zosh et al. 2018). It is important that teachers know the difference between planning an open-ended exploration that is "fun," but where little learning takes place, and offering an enjoyable, child-directed exploration that holds possibilities for deeper learning with skillful adult guidance, but where the teacher avoids intervening in or taking over the play.

The big idea here is that you don't have to choose between play or teaching academic skills, because, as Patricia McDonald explains in her book chapter about meeting standards through play, children "can meet and exceed standards through playful learning that combines open-ended experiences, child-directed initiatives, and teacher-guided activities" (2019, 25).

ESSENTIAL COMPONENTS OF AN INTENTIONALLY DESIGNED PLAYFUL LEARNING EXPERIENCE

Drawing on the definition and research outlined in part 1, I have outlined five critical components to consider when planning intentional playful learning experiences focused on spatial skills.

1. Design each exploration to be active, engaging, meaningful, socially interactive, iterative, and joyful.
2. Focus each exploration on a specific spatial skill and include elements known to foster spatial learning.
3. Incorporate strategies that guide deeper spatial learning during key moments of the exploration.
4. Plan additional opportunities that extend spatial learning within and outside the classroom.
5. Include developmentally appropriate assessments of spatial learning through observation and documentation.

1. Design Each Exploration to Be Active, Engaging, Meaningful, Socially Interactive, Iterative, and Joyful

Research scientists from the fields of psychology, education, neuroscience, and linguistics who studied optimal learning environments came to a consensus about key features they believe best foster children's learning (Hirsh-Pasek et al. in Zosh et al. 2018). Supported by the literature, these scientists confirmed that children learn best when the learning is "active, engaged, meaningful, socially interactive, iterative and joyful" (Zosh et al. 2018, 3). So what applications can we make to support learning spatial skills based on this research?

Active

In active explorations children do not sit passively absorbing information during whole-group instruction. Rather, they are highly engaged in the construction of knowledge through manipulation of materials and through a deeper processing of information in what I call "playful explorations." For example, the teacher does not show the children a triangle and say, "This is a triangle." Instead, teachers give children a variety of triangle shapes with sides of differing lengths and invite them to discover the secret, or *rule*, as they say in mathematics, to explain why they are all triangles. These playful explorations ideally occur throughout the day in classroom learning centers or outdoors, but the teacher can also intentionally plan an exploration during small-group time. The distinction is that in an active exploration, you will see "minds-on-thinking in an enjoyable and child-directed context" (Zosh et al. 2018, 4), which has been shown to help children retain information, especially when coupled with guided play.

Engaging

Children are deeply engaged in an exploration when they stay on task for extended periods of time. The ability to remain focused while ignoring distractions develops during childhood. Play naturally enables children to stay engaged, leading to increased executive function or self-regulation skills, which is one of the factors linked to early mathematics ability (Verdine et al. 2017). Guided play, where the teacher scaffolds learning toward a specific goal, such as spatial thinking skills, has been shown to maximize engagement, especially for young children who are easily distracted (Zosh et al. 2018).

Meaningful

Experienced teachers know that in order to capture a child's attention and encourage deeper engagement, playful exploration has to be meaningful. Deeper learning, especially as it applies to spatial thinking skills, requires that the learner not only store information but also connect it to prior, relevant information that they then transfer to new situations or problems. This highlights the importance of observing children during play to learn more about their interests to build on the "themes, objects, and people that are relevant and interesting to them" (Zosh et al. 2018, 5).

Socially interactive

One of the many benefits of play is that children learn social skills: how to enter play, how to take turns, and how to get along with others. We also want children to build on each other's knowledge as they work to achieve a goal in a socially interactive exploration. As children work collaboratively to solve a problem or complete a task, they are practicing many skills. Chi states that "building on each other's contribution, defending and arguing a position, challenging and criticizing each other on the same concept or point, asking and answering each other's questions" are all part of socialization (Chi in Zosh et al. 2018, 6).

Iterative

Learning is iterative when children actively explore materials to build new knowledge and then test and revise their ideas and theories with teacher guidance. Chalufour and Worth (2004, 68) describe a cycle of inquiry (see diagram on page 34) that begins with explorations that encourage children to engage, notice, wonder, and question through open-ended play, followed by more focused observations and clarifying questions. The next stage of the cycle is focused on an investigation or exploration as the teacher and children plan, predict, act, and then observe closely while collecting, recording, and representing experiences and data. They then reflect on the experience, explore patterns and relationships, construct reasonable explanations, and ask new questions. After reflection and discussion, they draw conclusions and formulate ideas and theories and start the process again.

More than just arriving at an answer, teachers must create a culture of inquiry that moves beyond merely transmitting information and instead focuses on the questions and a process for investigating them. As Pelo and Carter state, "A culture of inquiry values complexity, not-knowing, uncertainty, divergent and contradictory ideas" and "honors imagination and creative leaps, gestures of intuition and spirit

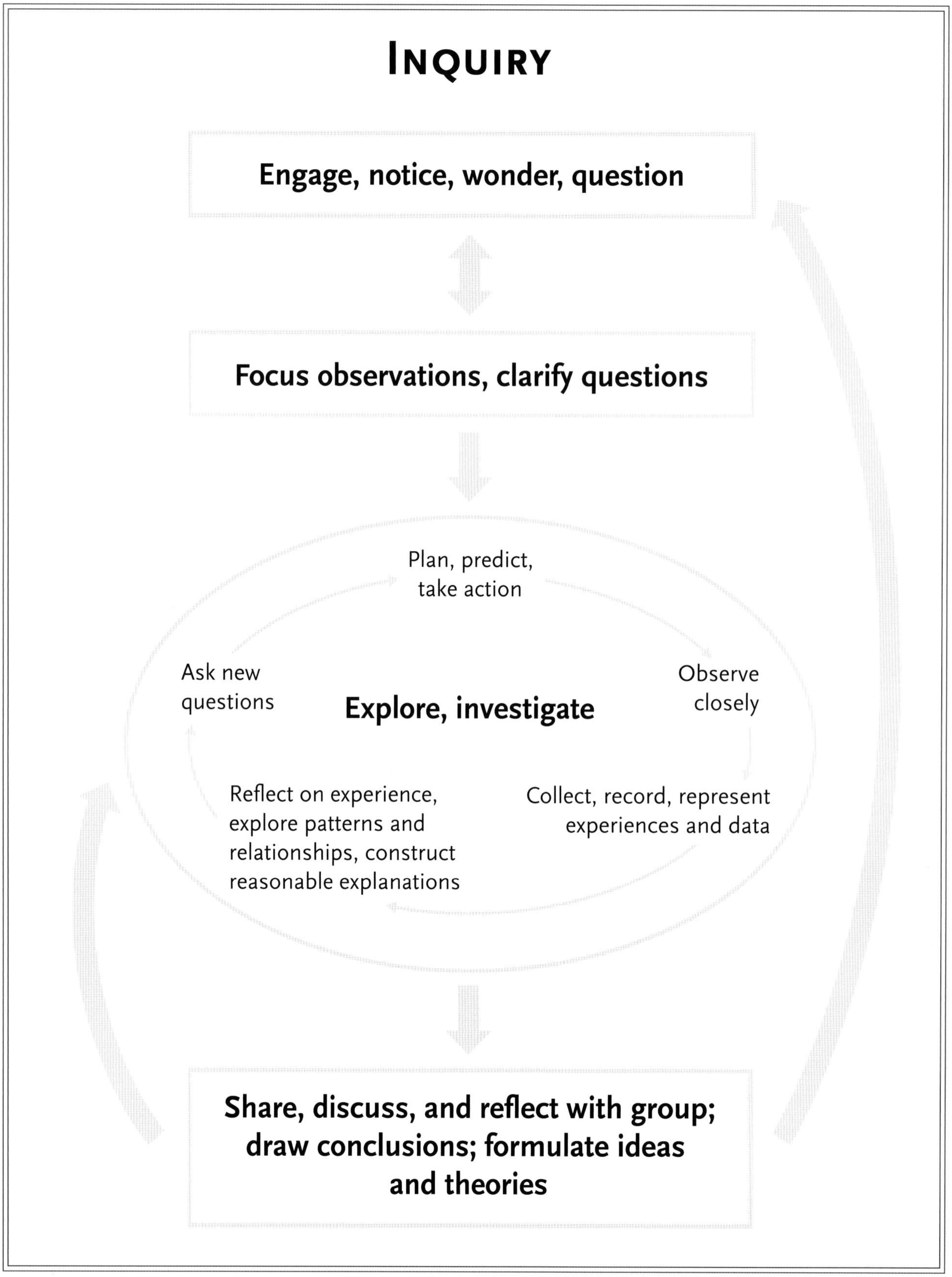

INQUIRY

Engage, notice, wonder, question

Focus observations, clarify questions

Plan, predict,
take action

Ask new
questions

Explore, investigate

Observe
closely

Reflect on experience,
explore patterns and
relationships, construct
reasonable explanations

Collect, record, represent
experiences and data

**Share, discuss, and reflect with group;
draw conclusions; formulate ideas
and theories**

Education Development Center 2004

and heart" (2018, 52–53). This type of playful exploration inspires iteration, and when supported by a teacher or adult, children can move toward more advanced types of theory testing (Zosh et al. 2018).

Joyful

Joy is a critical element of a playful exploration in which children feel positive emotions and interact with one another in constructive ways during experiences that require little outer motivation. Researchers studying play note that when learning is joyful it increases creativity, which is linked to increased learning. When playful explorations contain an element of surprise, curiosity is piqued, which also leads to greater learning (Zosh et al. 2018). It is encouraging to hear research scientists acknowledge the important role of joy in learning when the current focus seems to be on scripted curricula and rote standards-based learning. I believe we want children to be intrinsically motivated, curious, creative, and joyful when they are engaged in learning.

The following "Carnival" story from Mrs. Szczubelek's public kindergarten classroom beautifully illustrates a playful exploration that is active, engaging, meaningful, socially interactive, iterative, and joyful, while also incorporating spatial learning.

Mrs. Szczubelek explained that the carnival exploration started when her student Ansel built a carousel. "Look at the symmetrical patterns I made!" he exclaimed as he summoned her to the block center.

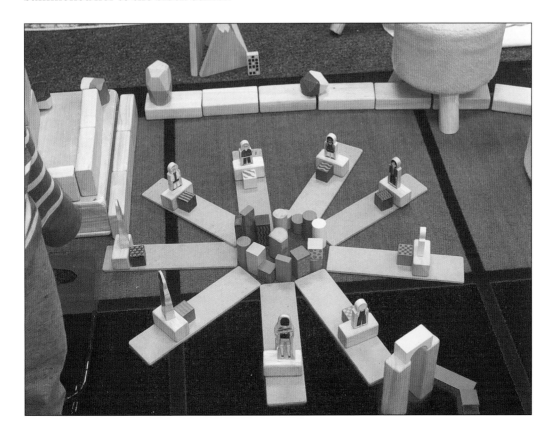

Lucianne overheard Ansel talking with Mrs. Szczubelek about the carousel and suggested a carnival with multiple paths, lights, and rides. Then Eli, Avery, and Amelia joined in.

Carnival entrance

Road to carnival

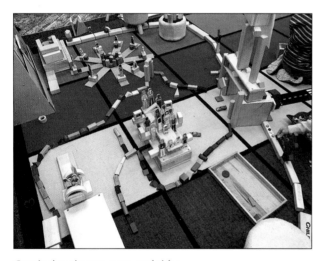

Carnival pathways, gate, and rides

Mrs. Szczubelek added, "We decided to let the children work on the carnival over a three-day period. We even moved our teaching spot so that they could do this. The children were using so many skills during this playful exploration: they were counting, patterning, balancing, judging capacity, and building an understanding of perspective taking and dimension shifting.

Patterns on a fence

Bird's-eye view of the carnival

"There were ten children working cooperatively on the carnival at one point. They then built a waterslide out of a ramp and were sending floats and people down the ramp. Each day it was getting more intricate and involved. It was really a sight to see! My colleague even brought her class in to see it in hopes it would inspire her class." Indeed, it did. The children in Mrs. Ciemniecki's class created their own theme park attractions.

Boat with passengers

Carousel bumper boats

2. Focus Each Exploration on a Specific Spatial Skill and Include Elements Known to Foster Spatial Learning

Because spatial skills tend to be neglected in early childhood education in general and mathematics in particular, it is important to intentionally plan to include a specific spatial skill or skills during each exploration. As we learned in part 1, spatial skills are not included in every math curriculum and children don't always learn spatial concepts during play. It is up to the adult to make sure that all children, including girls, children of color, dual-language learners, and those with learning disabilities, have opportunities to connect spatial concepts to the ideas they are exploring during their play.

Ensure that you have a clear understanding of the specific spatial skill you are introducing and are confident in guiding children as they learn it

Resources from the National Association for the Education of Young Children, the National Council of Teachers of Mathematics, the Office of Head Start, and your state's standards will provide specific guidelines on geometry and spatial skills for each age group.

If you need help in this area, seek out professional development opportunities at local or national conferences or connect with peers and form a professional learning community to increase your comfort level in teaching spatial skills. Renee Whelan, the early childhood director at a school district in New Jersey, describes the partnership she established with two organizations that assist teachers in supporting children's spatial and numeracy skills.

Dr. Renee Whelan, Director of Early Childhood, Long Branch Public Schools, New Jersey

"Long Branch Public Schools partnered with the New Jersey Department of Education in an early learning mathematics professional learning opportunity involving the Council of Chief State Officers. As we concentrated on improving our short- and long-term outcomes in mathematics, we focused on understanding how to support children's spatial skills in addition to numeracy.

"As the teachers became more familiar with the learning trajectories in this domain, their centers integrated more opportunities for children to explore spatial relationships. Additionally, the teachers dedicated a learning center that solely supported this development.

"During my classroom visits, I would watch the students build in their block center with Keva planks, create origami designs, draw maps, use tangrams to make pictures, and participate in other engaging spatial experiences. The teachers and I discussed differentiating the centers to scaffold each child's spatial sense. For instance, we noticed that the block center needed some engineering challenges and visual models to advance the children's spatial skills to the next level—some children would remain at a basic building level if this center were just a free-play center. Interactions between teachers and children also played a critical factor in this differentiating process. As we gained a better understanding of spatial sense through professional learning opportunities, the children's experiences became richer, more purposeful, and joyful! We are excited to see their positive learning outcomes and look forward to continuing to learn how best to support each child's spatial development as they progress from one grade to the next."

Offer materials, books, and visual representations to support spatial learning

As you introduce each new spatial skill, reinforce the ideas children are learning through books that explain or illustrate spatial concepts. For example, in the book *Zoom* by István Bányai, children are taken on a wordless visual journey to explore the idea of perspective taking. You will also discover many excellent books with spatial words in them that help children better understand spatial language. In the following chapters, I have included a list of recommended books that are focused on a specific spatial skill or skills.

Displaying drawings, blueprints, photographs, pictures, and other visual images in the classroom provides children with additional pathways to understanding concepts that are not always easily understood through verbal explanations alone. For example, you can create visual daily schedules that represent blocks of time that are correlated by length to the amount of time for each activity, reinforcing the idea that variations in spacing can have meaning in a graphic (Newcombe 2013). Today many classrooms include graphs that children have created with their teachers to represent collected data, such as which version of "The Three Little Pigs" they liked best out of the five the teacher read to them.

Hands-on experiences with materials such as blocks are essential for all children but may be particularly important for English-language learners and children with language delays. These children rely more on tactile and visual experiences with materials than experiences with language to develop geometric concepts (Kuder and Hojnoski 2018). Offering a wide variety of avenues for learning spatial skills throughout the day connected to all subjects and domains and during planned small-group activities or at learning centers is essential to fostering spatial skills.

3. Incorporate Strategies That Guide Deeper Spatial Learning during Key Moments of the Exploration

As children are engaged in a playful exploration, whether it is during a planned small-group activity, at a learning center, or outdoors, there is much the teacher or adult can do to respond to and support children's thinking pertaining to spatial skills.

Acknowledge effort and offer words of encouragement

A good place to begin is spending time observing what children are doing during the exploration. If they seem frustrated, you might start out by acknowledging their frustration without correcting them or solving the problem for them. Remember, math educators say it is important for children to make mistakes and learn from them. You might say, "You look frustrated that you don't know where that piece of the tangram puzzle goes. I see you have been turning and rotating the shapes to make them fit. That's a great start! It will get easier with practice."

Describe and expand on what children do and say

Describing what children are doing is as simple as putting words to what you observe. For example, "I noticed that you, Julio, and Lyla have been working together to re-create the zoo out of blocks using the map of the zoo." When using such "parallel talk," you take on the role of broadcaster, narrating what a child is doing in real time. By doing so, you describe the moment in detail, sometimes taking the opportunity to use targeted vocabulary. You can also expand on ideas the children have by asking for descriptive details, examples, comparisons, or alternatives. For example, "When we visited the zoo, was the enclosure for the elephants next to or behind the enclosure for the giraffes? Can you show me where they are in your construction?"

Ask open-ended questions

Open-ended questions are those that require more thought than just a simple one-word answer. It's tempting to want to lead children to the "correct" answer but important to remember that the question should encourage children to think of different possibilities. For example, "I see that the cars and trucks don't fit inside the parking garage you constructed. What can you do to fix the garage so that they all fit inside?" We have included a list of suggested questions for each chapter in part 2, but it is better when teachers give their full attention to the ideas children are exploring to carefully craft

each question. You will often see children walk away from their playful investigation when they feel bombarded by too many questions. Learning the art of inquiry takes great skill and practice. An excellent resource for sharpening your questioning techniques with young children can be found in the book *Big Questions for Young Minds* (Strasser and Bresson 2017).

Use and encourage specific spatial language and gestures

As we learned in chapter 2, teaching and modeling specific spatial language, especially when children are exploring with materials like blocks, supports children in improving their spatial abilities. This can include naming the shapes children are using in their constructions or describing the positions of the blocks. For example, "I see you put all the cylinders *next to* each other and arranged the quarter circle blocks *on top of* them."

Children may use hand gestures to communicate directions such as left and right or high and low when they don't have the words to explain what they know. When adults are looking at a shape with a child and point to a corner as they say "corner," they are using gestures to foster spatial knowledge (Cartmill et al. in Verdine et al. 2017).

Point out spatial elements, concepts, and new terms

Although teachers can introduce new concepts in a large group setting using a story or by verbally explaining a term, children learn spatial language and new spatial concepts and terms in context while they are actually exploring the properties of materials and what they can do in real time. For example, if a child is having a difficult time getting started with a puzzle, you might say, "Remember the straight edge goes around the outside," or remind them to turn pieces around in their hands if it doesn't fit on the first try.

Make connections with other areas of learning and life

What better way to learn about shapes in the built environment than by going for a neighborhood walk? When teachers create playful explorations that include children's families, communities, and interests, it sparks their motivation to learn and helps them make connections that are meaningful. For example, as children walk through their school's neighborhood, they can identify two-dimensional shapes like triangles, circles, squares, and rectangles, and three-dimensional shapes such as spheres, cubes, rectangular prisms, pyramids, cylinders, and cones in the buildings, vehicles, signs, and sidewalks they see. This is also a great way to incorporate the active, physical exploration of the real world that helps children make connections with their bodies in space.

Encourage multiple ways for children to express their ideas and thinking

There are many ways children can convey their understanding of a spatial concept besides gestures and written or verbal explanations. Children may not be able to explain what an ABAB pattern is, for example, but they may be able to show you how they create an original pattern or extend an already existing pattern with authentic materials such as blocks, modeling clay, buttons, keys, or sticks. Chapter 10 provides useful strategies for guiding children in expressing their ideas through drawing.

Honor the pace of each child

As we learned in chapter 2, learning math, and spatial skills in particular, is not a race. If we want children to learn basic spatial skills more deeply, we have to acknowledge their level of understanding and not worry about pacing guides that don't gauge the individual child's stage of development. Not every child will be at the same point at the same time, which is why large-group instruction is not as effective for teaching children as is providing age-appropriate activities in small groups and learning centers with adult support.

Provide time for reflection

Reflection is a process for remembering and thinking about what you have learned. Adults can encourage reflection by giving children opportunities to communicate their ideas and thoughts during or after the playful exploration through drawing, writing, singing, acting out, sharing, and talking. Visual documentation, discussed in chapter 10, is an excellent way for children to revisit their work. This reflection process helps children connect what they learn to other situations and helps teachers to reevaluate their instruction and make changes to improve their teaching (Nell, Drew, and Bush 2013).

Model and coach respectful listening and sharing

Whether in a large- or small-group setting, it is important for teachers to create a culture and climate of respect where children's ideas and contributions are valued and can be shared. A good place to start is to model for children what it means to show respect for a speaker: look at the speaker, be quiet when the person is speaking, and ask thoughtful questions. At times it may be necessary to teach children the difference between a question and a comment, remind children not to interrupt the speaker, or help children who monopolize a discussion learn how to give others a turn to speak. Some children may need gentle reminders to stay on point or to project their voices so they can be heard. When children are eager to share all at once or too timid to share in a large group, pairing them with partners allows everyone to speak and listen. Recording questions or observations on chart paper or on a touch pad lets children know their ideas are important.

4. Plan Additional Opportunities That Extend Spatial Learning within and outside the Classroom

Active, self-directed learning in classroom centers offers children the freedom and time to explore their personal interests while developing spatial skills and interacting with peers. When this is supplemented with parent engagement in the classroom and at home, spatial skills are reinforced in a meaningful way.

Create learning centers that target specific spatial skills

Setting up learning centers with materials suited for spatial learning can reinforce specific spatial skills while also offering children different choices and approaches to learning. Organizing the center so that the materials can be easily seen and independently accessed will make it far more likely that they will be used. Each of the chapters in part 2 offers ideas for enhancing your learning centers so they include targeted spatial skills.

Offer appropriate learning experiences that can be done at home

Giving children experiential activities to do at home that improve spatial understanding is far superior to worksheets or workbook activities. Suggest that parents can do activities like puzzles alongside older children, while younger children can explore how objects take up space when they are placed in a larger container. Walks in nature or around the neighborhood allow adults to describe positions, directions, and distances using specific spatial language. Encourage parents to visit local museums, libraries, and playgrounds with their children. Suggestions for experiences that support spatial learning at home are included in the following chapters.

Invite parents and community members to share interests or expertise

Welcome parents and community members into your classroom to share stories about how they use spatial skills in their work or home. Some may be willing to demonstrate a spatial concept they use in a hobby, game, or sport.

5. Include Developmentally Appropriate Assessments of Spatial Learning through Observation and Documentation

It is important to reflect on the playful exploration you planned and whether children understood the spatial concept you intended for them to learn. Questions you should ask yourself are:

What specific spatial skill did this playful exploration teach?

Did every child become playfully and deeply engaged in the exploration? What evidence supports this?

What spatial skills did each child learn? How do you know?

What might you do to expand or fine-tune the exploration to ensure children understand the spatial skills you have introduced?

As discussed earlier, there are few reliable tests that accurately convey what young children know and understand about multiple spatial concepts. Observing what children are doing as they are engaged in the exploration, noticing if they are using spatial language accurately, and actively documenting their actions, comments, questions, and answers to your questions, while taking photos of their work, will provide the best evidence of what they have learned. You will see where individual children are struggling and need support and where children have mastered concepts and are ready for new challenges. While you will be focused on spatial skill development in these observations, you will also be looking at other areas of development to see how they fit together, giving you a complete picture of the whole child.

Chapters 4–10 define specific spatial skills and highlight each with examples from early childhood classrooms. Examples in these chapters may not include all the components detailed here, but they are a great place to start. What's important is to strive to make spatial skills an essential component in each playful exploration.

Geometric Shapes and Properties

We can give children an important start in their spatial development by having them recognize, name, and describe basic geometric shapes when they are developmentally ready, typically between the ages of three and five.

Shape Vocabulary

Two-dimensional (2-D) shapes:

Circle (no angles, rounded edge)

Triangle (3 angles, 3 sides)

Rectangle (4 right angles, 4 sides)

Square or squared rectangle (4 right angles, same length/congruent sides)

Pentagon (5 sides, 5 angles)

Hexagon (6 sides, 6 angles)

Octagon (8 sides, 8 angles)

Rhombus (diamond shaped: 4 angles, opposite sides parallel)

Trapezoid (a quadrilateral with 1 pair of parallel sides)

Curved line (open curve)

Angle (2 lines that meet to make a corner or vertex)

Right angle (2 lines that meet to make a corner measuring 90 degrees)

Congruent (exactly alike in shape and size, can be superimposed)

Parallel lines (lines that remain the same distance apart, like railroad tracks)

Parallelogram (quadrilateral with 2 pairs of opposite parallel sides)

Plane (a flat surface)

Shape (2-D or 3-D geometric figure made up of points, lines, or planes)

Quadrilateral (a polygon with 4 straight sides)

Polygon (a plane figure bounded by 3 or more straight sides)

Continued on next page.

Shape Vocabulary (continued)

Three-dimensional (3-D) shapes:

Cube (squared faces, 6 surfaces)

Sphere (rounded surface)

Cone (circular base that is connected to a single point over the base, creating a curved surface)

Cylinder (circular ends, rounded sides)

Rectangular solid or prism (rectangular faces, 6 surfaces)

Pyramid (polygon base that is connected to a single point over the base, with triangles)

(Schwartz 2005; Clements and Sarama 2014)

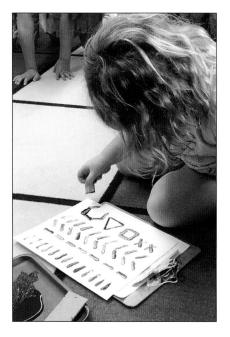

LINES MAKE SHAPES

As children paint, draw, and print, they readily identify and explore lines, eventually discovering that lines make shapes. Line printing is a simple way for children to explore vertical, horizontal, diagonal, and curved lines (and when ready, even parallel and perpendicular lines) using the side of a rectangular piece of corrugated cardboard or circular cardboard (from the inside of a roll of masking tape, for example) dipped in paint.

The perfect time to expand the children's geometrical vocabulary and explain the attributes of the shapes is when they begin to make shapes from lines. For example, "I see you made a shape with three equal sides and you said it was a triangle. That's right! But did you know that triangles can also have sides that aren't the same length? Here are three different sizes of cardboard. Can you show me how you can make different triangle shapes with them?"

Making large geometric shapes with connector rods, making outlines on geoboards, or creating shapes out of straws, molding clay coils, pipe cleaners, or wire are other ways that children

can begin to understand how shapes are made. In geometry, two-dimensional shapes are made up of lines and three-dimensional shapes are made up of planes, faces, or surfaces.

CLASSIFY AND SORT SHAPES

Many games and activities are designed to help children classify and sort shapes. Starting with classic shape-sorting toys for toddlers, by trial and error and eventually with more attuned spatial skills, a child learns to place 3-D shapes into the correct shaped hole. Sorting can later advance to stacking 3-D shapes (largest on bottom, smallest on top) or lining up boxes, shapes, or cylinders horizontally by size or color.

Games in which children compare the characteristics of shapes or match shapes by how many sides or vertices they have help build geometric vocabulary and shape knowledge.

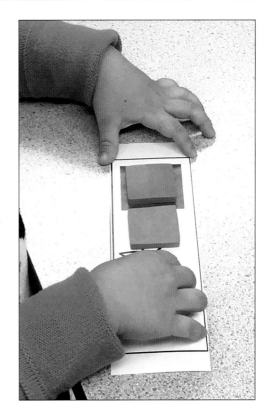

Children work in pairs to place the cylinder blocks in order so that in each column or row a color appears just once.

In this activity, children arrange nine blocks on a 3 x 3 wooden grid. The blocks come in three colors (yellow, green, and orange) and three shapes (square, pentagon, and hexagon), so there is one block of each possible color and shape combination. For example, there is a yellow square, a green square, and an orange square. The blocks are put on the 3 x 3 grid in a special order. All three blocks in a row or column should be either the same color or the same shape. For instance, blocks in the first column should all be yellow or all be square.

In shape sudoku, children work with different shapes on a grid, making sure no shapes are repeated in a row or column.

In color sudoku, children are given a set of unit squares in different colors: red, green, yellow, and blue. The children play sudoku with those squares, this time making sure no color is repeated in a row and a column.

Active exploration that is accompanied by adult guidance through targeted questions or prompts has been found to be especially beneficial for learning geometric shapes (Newcombe and Frick 2010, 107). Even young children can begin to generate strategies to explain why two shapes are the same or different. One excellent illustration of this is from the book *Which One Doesn't Belong? A Shapes Book* by Christopher Danielson (2016). Readers are presented with four shapes, asked which one is different, and then asked to explain why. With teacher guidance, this challenging task prompts lively conversations, sophisticated reasoning, and precise spatial language. Children are delighted to find that there is no one correct answer!

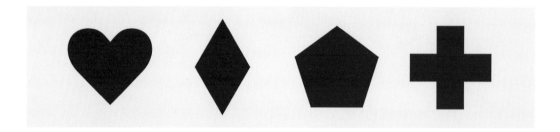

USING SHAPES TO JUDGE CAPACITY, VOLUME, AND MAGNITUDE

Children experiment with the mathematical concepts of capacity, volume, and magnitude throughout the day. The ability to judge capacity grows during complex construction play, such as when children construct a parking garage out of blocks or magnetic tiles. Through this activity, they demonstrate their skill at making adjustments to accommodate the number and sizes of cars they have on hand . . .

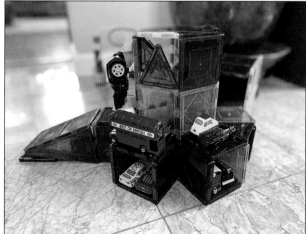

or create a structure that could fit all the children in the classroom...

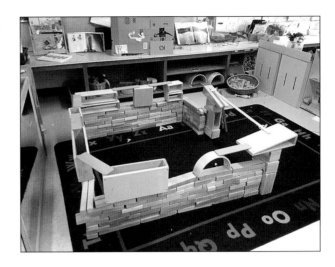

or passages for people or their vehicles to pass through.

On a number line, children can use blocks to help them visualize the concept of magnitude, thereby connecting numeracy concepts such as the number line to spatial and geometry concepts (Schwartz 2017), or make visual comparisons using a variety of objects. Measurement activities such as these present a range of learning opportunities that require and engage spatial thinking (Ontario Ministry 2014). In Kelly Bhatia's kindergarten classroom, the children identified a problem and applied their measurement and spatial skills to build a trap out of magnetic tiles.

**Mrs. Kelly Bhatia, Kindergarten Teacher,
Scotch Plains–Fanwood Regional School District, New Jersey**

"After hearing a rumor of the existence of a mouse, the children spent two days measuring and building this trap using magnetic tiles. They did some research to find the distance that a mouse can jump and, within the structure, built levels that the mouse would fall into, but not be able to jump out of, based on this distance. In the center is a piece of cheese stick from snack.

"The children realized that if they made the base narrower, they would have more tiles available to make it taller."

LEARNING CENTERS

Block Center

Set up the block area to give children opportunities to use blocks to judge capacity and volume. They can ask themselves how many blocks can fit into the container or on the shelf. As children return blocks to the shelves or containers marked with the respective shapes, they will be engaged in classifying and sorting the 3-D shapes to correspond with 2-D shapes.

When children build bridges, they learn to judge the distance between the block supports they are connecting.

Shape Play

Create a center with design templates and pattern blocks for children to work on independently or in pairs. Children place each pattern block shape on the template until the design is complete, learning the properties of 2-D shapes and practicing mental rotation.

Shape Printing

Set out different color paints brushed evenly on small paper plates and provide a variety of boxes or other objects to press into the paint and print onto paper to create 2-D shapes.

Sand Table

Offer natural materials, such as field corn, sand, acorns, small pine cones, or water, with a variety of containers so children can experiment with quantity and volume while also learning the properties of materials.

Dramatic Play Center

Encourage children to build enclosures, such as homes for different animals and dolls, making adjustments to accommodate various sizes. Use spatial language to point out concepts of size, and use nonstandard items for measurement.

Light Table

If you don't already have a light table in your classroom, consider purchasing or requesting one of the many inexpensive table-top models found in school supply catalogs. You can also find simple directions for making your own online (see, for example, www .pre-kpages.com/diy-light-table). Invite children to play with transparent 2-D pattern blocks or 3-D blocks on the light table.

Overhead Projector Explorations

Use an overhead projector (sitting unused in many school closets, looking for adoption) to cast transparent shapes onto mural paper or an erasable whiteboard, and invite the children to trace the shapes with markers or their fingers.

SPATIAL SKILLS AND VOCABULARY

- Shape Vocabulary (see box pages 45–46)
- Lines: vertical, horizontal, diagonal, curved, perpendicular, parallel

QUESTIONS AND CONVERSATION STARTERS TO EXPAND LEARNING

- How is that shape like this one? How is it different?
- Why isn't this shape an [oval]? What makes it a [circle]?
- Where have you seen this shape before?
- Can you think of another name for this shape?
- What shape could you make out of these shapes?
- I wonder how you might make a shape with . . . (straw connectors, pipe cleaner, playdough, wire)?
- I notice that you . . .
- I wonder if . . .
- How might you . . . ?

EXPERIENTIAL ACTIVITIES TO TRY AT HOME

- Recommend books about shapes that families can read with their children.
- Suggest sorting games with found objects, shapes, and pattern blocks.

- Provide fun ideas for going on a neighborhood or around-the-house shape hunt. Suggest that parents use a tablet or phone to photograph both simple shapes and shapes within shapes, such as the center of a flower head, a close-up of a doorknob, or window panes within a window, then have children identify and name the shapes.
- To limit the use of electronic devices, suggest using a magnetic tangram set or magnetic wooden block set. Sometimes all you need is a piece of paper, a pencil, and good observation skills.

While waiting for her sister's dance lessons to conclude, instead of indulging in more screen time, Ellie's mother encourages her to discover patterns in architecture, find shapes inside of other shapes, or notice how two shapes make another shape. Here Ellie is searching for circles inside the building and then tallying the total in her shape hunt notebook.

- Share parent websites that provide ideas for supporting spatial and math skills, such as:
  - www.pbs.org/parents/thrive/spatial-skills-the-secret-ingredient-to -childrens-stem-success
  - www.pbs.org/parents/learn-grow/age-5/math/spatial-skills
  - www.naeyc.org/our-work/for-families
  - www.stmath.com
  - https://parents.britannica.com
  - https://tinkergarten.com
- On her Parenting Science website, www.parentingscience.com/spatial-skills .html, Gwen Dewar (2016) offers a list of questions parents can ask children to engage them in conversations, such as:
  - *Which way does the sheet fit on the bed?*
  - *Will the groceries fit in one bag?*
  - *Which shapes do I get if I cut my bagel the other way—and will it still fit in the toaster?*

CHILDREN'S BOOKS: GEOMETRIC SHAPES AND PROPERTIES

R. L. Allington, *Shapes*

Joan Sullivan Baranski, *Round Is a Pancake*

April Barth, *Building with Solid Shapes*

Paula Bossio, *The Line*

Marilyn Burns, *The Greedy Triangle*

Eric Carle, *The Secret Birthday Message*

Michael J. Crosbie, *Architecture Shapes*

Christopher Danielson, *Which One Doesn't Belong? A Shapes Book*

Dayle Ann Dodds, *The Shape of Things*

Rhonda Growler Greene, *When a Line Bends . . . a Shape Begins*

Tana Hoban, *Circles, Triangles and Squares*

Tana Hoban, *Push, Pull, Empty, Full: A Book of Opposites*

Tana Hoban, *Round and Round and Round*

Tana Hoban, *Shapes, Shapes, Shapes*

Tana Hoban, *Shapes and Things*

Tana Hoban, *So Many Circles, So Many Squares*

Tana Hoban, *Spirals, Curves, Fanshapes & Lines*

Elizabeth and Douglas MacAgy, *Going for a Walk with a Line*

Suse MacDonald, *Sea Shapes*

Mineko Mamada, *Which Is Round? Which Is Bigger?*

Catherine Rayner, *Ernest, the Moose Who Doesn't Fit*

Noemie Revah and Olimpia Zagnoli, *Mister Horizontal & Miss Vertical*

Marisabina Russo, *The Line Up Book*

Carole Lexa Schaefer, *The Squiggle*

Danile Shepard, *Solid Shapes*

Roseanne Thong, *Round Is a Mooncake: A Book of Shapes*

Roseanne Thong, *Round Is a Tortilla: A Book of Shapes*

Candace Whitman, *Lines That Wiggle*

Philip Yenawine, *Lines*

Philip Yenawine, *Shapes*

Patterns

As the 2008 National Mathematics Advisory Panel concluded that patterns were no longer a topic of major importance and the 2010 Common Core State Standards ignored spatial skills and pushed learning symmetrical patterns to the later grades, early patterning activities dropped out of favor. Today there is general agreement that preschool children's patterning and spatial skills predict their future math achievement (Rittle-Johnson, Zippert, and Boice 2018; Sarama and Clements 2004; Cheng and Mix 2013) and that early math education should be expanded to incorporate more patterning and spatial skills. Not all research specifically includes patterning as a spatial skill, but successful patterning requires both visual-spatial skills and numerical reasoning.

Many early childhood teachers report that they frequently see children engaging in patterning during play. In my work providing professional development in math for teachers, I have observed this as well, but I noticed that the patterning activities rarely included the more sophisticated patterns that might be encouraged with adult support. Thus, this chapter is included to provide additional ideas for classroom and home explorations on patterning.

LINEAR AND RADIAL PATTERNS

Children are natural patternmakers and readily find materials in the environment to create linear patterns.

 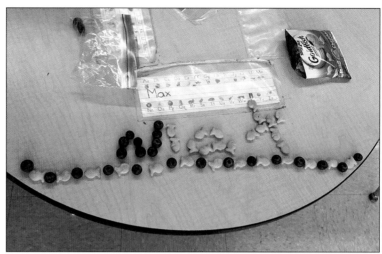

Objects can be arranged to follow a pattern; in mathematical terms, they are arranged according to a rule. For example, the rule for this linear pattern is that a triangle will follow two squares:

Teachers can build on this interest by offering unit cubes for children to explore the rule of a given pattern, to find the next shape in a given pattern, and to make a new pattern. In the photo below, children work on forming a pattern described by the teachers. Later in the same activity the children are given time to design their own patterns. Children are invited to share their work with each other.

Taking the idea of line printing from chapter 4, children were shown how to dip corrugated cardboard rectangles into a thin layer of paint and then invited to create interesting linear patterns with repeating horizontal, vertical, and diagonal lines and shapes.

Children can also experiment with radial designs, which build on patterning concepts. These designs start at a center point and fan out like spokes on a wheel and often include a natural symmetrical design.

Creating a true radial pattern can be challenging for young children, but as you learned in the story of Daraja in chapter 2, children love to take on new challenges.

Making linear and radial patterns using line printing

TESSELLATIONS

A tessellation is created when a shape is repeated over and over again, covering an area with no space between the shapes.

Elliana demonstrates making a tessellation with line printing while her teacher observes.

Taylor creates a tessellation with pattern blocks.

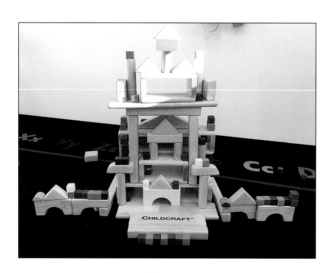

SYMMETRY

Sarama and Clements note that children frequently incorporate symmetry in their free play, especially when playing with blocks (in Moss et al. 2016, 20). While not all result in exact mirror images, you will notice that children have a surprising ability to design with symmetry.

Two shapes are symmetric if you can slide, flip, or turn one of them to match the other side exactly, as if you were seeing its reflection in a mirror. An important mathematical concept children learn when they are introduced to transformation is reflection (more on this in chapter 6). Provide children with half-finished pattern block designs on one side of a line of symmetry and challenge them to create a symmetric design by placing matching blocks on the other side of the line in correct orientations. This activity will help them get started with making symmetrical patterns (Moss et al. 2016).

The following vignette is a good example of how a teacher can sit with a child during free play or choice time to observe the child's understanding of a concept and to provide clarification, if needed.

Mrs. Kelly Bhatia, Kindergarten Teacher, Scotch Plains–Fanwood Regional School District, New Jersey

"Following a math lesson on symmetry, Cara went to the choice center I had set up in the classroom with items offered to encourage further exploration of symmetry.

"I noticed Cara busy in the center with some air-dry clay and a pile of unfinished wooden pieces of different sizes and shapes.

"When I went to visit Cara at the center, she said she was making a 'symmetry butterfly.'

"I listened carefully as Cara elaborated by sharing some of the observations we had made about patterns found in nature and tried to prove its symmetry by pointing out the matching shapes on opposite sides, making 'both sides look the same.'

"Because Cara had introduced two lines of symmetry, I pointed out that she had done a great job of making sure her wooden shapes were symmetrical on both sides of each line. If she had not done that, this would have been an opportunity to question her understanding of symmetry."

LEARNING CENTERS

Block Center

Post visuals or provide a notebook filled with images of patterns in tiles, textiles, and carpets from different cultures to inspire children to experiment with creating tessellations and linear and radial patterns with blocks. As children are building, point out 2-D or 3-D patterns that emerge.

Art Center

Take a photo of each child's face, cut the photo in half lengthwise, and glue it to a sheet of drawing paper on the line of symmetry (folding the drawing paper in half lengthwise is an easy way to center the photo on the paper). Invite children to use colored pencils or markers to draw the missing half of their face. The result is a symmetrical portrait!

Line Printing Station

Once you have demonstrated how to make patterns using the line printing technique, set up a small paper plate with a thin layer of tempera paint. Cut various sizes of rectangles from corrugated cardboard. You can also include toilet paper or wrapping paper rolls that are cut in two-inch lengths or longer to make circles, or cut in half to make semicircles or curved lines. Provide recycled blank paper or inexpensive newsprint paper in various sizes. Give children time to experiment with the technique, then encourage them to explore a variety of linear patterns, such as ABAB, ABBA, ABCABC, and so forth.

Symmetry Partner Game

In this game, children work in pairs with pattern blocks. Each child takes turns placing a pattern block on one side of a line of symmetry, then challenges their partner to match the pattern by positioning an identical block on the other side of the line of symmetry.

Pattern Block Design Center

After introducing various types of patterns, provide pattern blocks on a table and invite children to create their own patterns. Offering graph paper for children to align their patterns adds a challenge for those who are ready. To scaffold children who need help getting started, display visuals that include step-by-step photos of various shapes or outlines to copy.

SPATIAL SKILLS AND VOCABULARY

- Linear patterns
- Radial patterns
- Tessellations
- Symmetrical patterns
- Reflection
- Mirror
- Congruent

QUESTIONS AND CONVERSATION STARTERS TO EXPAND LEARNING

- What shape or shapes should come next to make a linear pattern?
- How can you tell if both sides are symmetrical?
- How did you rotate the blocks to make a symmetrical pattern?
- Tell me about the pattern you made with the colored beads on your string.
- Which pattern was trickiest, the linear or radial pattern?
- Is the pattern you made with blocks the same as Xander's?

EXPERIENTIAL ACTIVITIES TO TRY AT HOME

- Recommend that families go on neighborhood walks to find patterns in nature and in the built environment.
- Give simple instructions for how to fold paper in half to make cuts so that when the paper is opened, a symmetrical shape is created.
- Suggest going on a "pattern hunt" at home.
- Share ideas for creating patterns with blocks or objects from around the house.

CHILDREN'S BOOKS: PATTERNS

Jacqueline Briggs Martin, *Snowflake Bentley*

Nancy Carlstrom, Jesse Bear series

Barbar Juster Ebenson and Helen Davie, *Echoes for the Eye: Poems to Celebrate Patterns in Nature*

Trudy Harris, *Pattern Bugs*

Trudy Harris *Pattern Fish*

Tana Hoban, *Over, Under and Through*

Bill Martin Jr., *Brown Bear, Brown Bear, What Do You See?*

Stuart Murphy, *A Pair of Socks*

Laura Numeroff, If You Give series

Marion Smoothey, *Shape Patterns (Let's Investigate)*

Walter Wick, *A Drop of Water: A Book of Science and Wonder*

Audrey Wood, *The Napping House*

Irene Yates, *All about Pattern*

Transforming, Composing, and Decomposing

Piaget stated that "to know an object . . . is not simply to look at it and make a mental copy or image of it. To know an object is to act on it. To know is to modify, to transform the object, and to understand the process of this transformation, and as a consequence to understand the way the object is constructed" (in Zosh et al. 2018, 7). Very young children get to know an object through all of their senses. For example, when babies are first introduced to three-dimensional blocks, they might first taste the block and decide that it's not food or that it is solid.

With continued exploration they discover that blocks have hard edges and that some shapes stack better than others.

Giving children ample time and opportunity for open-ended play with two- and three-dimensional objects allows them to physically transform the objects as they combine and take them apart or fit them together. These playful experiences with transforming, composing, and decomposing shapes and objects lays the foundation for mental transformation, which we will explore in the next chapter on visualization.

PUZZLES

Children use the mathematical idea of transformation when they turn, rotate, slide, or flip a shape as they play with tangram puzzles. A tangram is a set of seven geometric shapes—five triangles, a square, and a parallelogram—that form a square, but they can also be used to create an infinite number of other shapes.

Challenging children to create images using a puzzle template gives them a similar experience in turning, rotating, sliding, and flipping two-dimensional shapes. In the photo to the right, children are given several shapes from a tangram puzzle and are asked to create a square with two tangram pieces. They are also asked to create rectangles and triangles. When they have more experience with composition, they will be asked to make a square with three tangram pieces.

Doing jigsaw puzzles predicts good spatial thinking, especially when spatial language is modeled by adults (Newcombe 2010). The National Council of Teachers of Mathematics suggests that children in pre-K up to the second grade should have opportunities to "investigate and predict the results of putting together and taking apart two-dimensional shapes" (NCTM in Moss et al. 2016, 21).

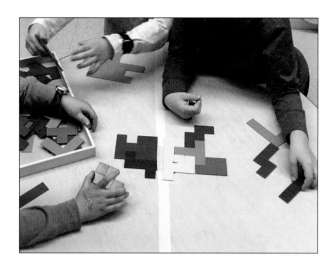

Pentominoes (geometric figures formed by joining five equal squares edge to edge) offer additional opportunities for composing and decomposing shapes.

In this exploration, children are given a set of pentominoes and, with the help of the teacher, are asked to form geometric shapes such as a rectangle or square using several pentomino pieces.

PAPER FOLDING

Paper folding, or origami, is an easy way to provide children practice with transforming shapes. Young children can start with folding a square in half to see that it makes a triangle, moving on to more challenging folds as they master shape-making (Pollman 2010). Spatial transformation skills learned from activities like these can lead to better performance on mathematical problems that require spatial representations, such as $2 + x = 5$ (Newcombe 2013).

In this photo, a teacher leads children in folding a sheet of paper to obtain a particular shape, such as a square, rectangle, or triangle. The teacher can also demonstrate how to make a rabbit or mouse using geometrical and spatial language while guiding the children. For example, she could say, "fold along the diagonal," "two congruent triangles," "a square on another one," and "the triangles are symmetrical."

WOODEN BLOCKS

Today there are a wide variety of blocks on the market. The unit blocks referred to here were first introduced by Caroline Pratt in the United States in the early twentieth century and inspired by German educator, mathematician, and architect Friedrich Fröbel, who is known as the father of kindergarten. Unit blocks are usually rectangular, made of wood, and measure about 5 x 1 x 2.5 inches. They come in sets with half, double, and quadruple units, although additional shapes are available.

As children progress in their block play, using their senses to explore the properties of blocks and composing and decomposing with them, they become more skilled at describing geometric attributes and properties and seeing how blocks are similar and different. These experiences provide a better understanding of such properties as congruence and symmetry (NCTM in Pollman 2010) as well as spatial visualization, spatial orientation, planning, and problem solving (Golbeck 2005). The children in the following photos have added large hollow blocks to their construction.

Wooden nature blocks, planks, and other wooden materials offer additional opportunities for spatial planning and problem solving.

In addition to working with wooden blocks, children can benefit from transforming, composing, and decomposing with other materials, such as magnetic tiles, pattern blocks, construction rods, cardboard, modeling clay, and a variety of natural and recycled materials or loose parts.

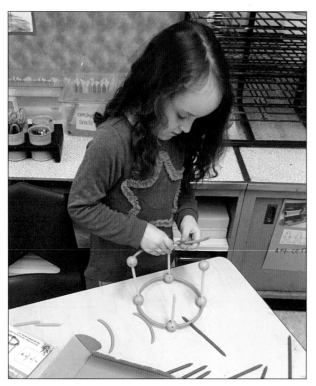

DECOMPOSING AND COMPOSING USING LITERATURE

In Ursus Wehrli's book *Tidying Up Art*, famous works of art are broken down, or decomposed, by color, shape, or other criteria and rearranged into a new composition. For example, the square shapes in Paul Klee's *Color Table* are decomposed and reassembled in stacks of squares arranged by color. The blue shapes in a work of art by Henri Matisse are decomposed and recomposed from largest to smallest.

As demonstrated in the following story provided by Krista Crumrine, children's literature is an excellent way to introduce math topics such as transforming, decomposing, and composing shapes.

Mrs. Krista Crumrine, Kindergarten Teacher, Union City School District, New Jersey

"In my kindergarten classroom, the children read Three Pigs, One Wolf, and Seven Magic Shapes *by Grace Maccarone. Following the story, children worked in small groups to make the animals from the story using the shapes from a tangram puzzle. They also enjoyed creating their own shapes.*

"Aliyah created a swan.

"Sebastian worked on a rabbit.

"Alisa and Sophia experimented with tangrams and worked together to make a rectangle. They created this on their own after making a square that was demonstrated in the story."

DECOMPOSING AND COMPOSING USING TECHNOLOGY

There are a number of good computer or video games, such as Tetris and Marble Madness, that may support spatial development, but researchers believe that there is not enough evidence that suggests they have a positive impact on children's spatial skills (Verdine et al. 2017). A computer screen is still two-dimensional, and young children need opportunities to use all their senses to manipulate and transform shapes that even the best software programs can't offer.

Research suggests that some electronic digital spatial toys might not be as good as nondigital toys for developing spatial skills (Zosh et al. 2015 in Berkowicz and Myers 2017). For example, they found that adults used more spatial language when children manipulated a traditional shape sorter, but when children played with the electronic version, adults focused more on button pushing and spoke less about the shapes. But when technology offers elements of light, sound, and color while also including concrete materials, body movement, and challenging tasks, imagine the possibilities!

In the Boulder Journey School's digi studio, children are offered natural materials to explore with technology. In the photograph at left, two prekindergarten-age children compose and decompose with natural materials on a light table. The light table adds elements of contrast and shadow to their exploration of composition.

Manipulating light through the variables of color and positioning offers opportunities for constructing and deconstructing new landscapes of light and shadow. A preschool-age child constructs new worlds through light and shadow in in these photos.

Three-dimensional materials are placed between a projector and a screen for children to manipulate, allowing them to explore space through physical interactions and providing a constructive and creative experience. In the photograph at right, three toddlers explore composition using loose parts in front of a projection. Adding mirrors to the experience heightens their depth and perspective.

LEARNING CENTERS

Block Center

At morning circle time introduce the idea of transforming shapes by rotating, sliding, or flipping three blocks. At center time encourage children to make as many combinations of shapes as they can with four or five blocks. Take photos or draw the constructed shape combinations and post them in the block center. Reinforce math and spatial language during this exploration. Remember to provide all children with equal opportunities to use the block center. Hands-on experiences with blocks are particularly important for English-language learners and children with language delays who may learn spatial concepts more easily by tactile and visual experiences with blocks than with language.

Origami Paper-Folding Center

Provide squares of lightweight paper and visual examples of simple folds. Show how to transform a square into many different shapes and animals. Include books on origami to inspire those who want to attempt more challenging folds.

Woodworking Center

Using a variety of authentic tools, wood, and other materials, create a center for construction and deconstruction. The materials and tools can be kept locked up until an adult is available to supervise.

Tangram Center

Create a center where children can place tangram puzzle pieces on an outline shape, or have children create their own shapes.

Math Manipulatives Center

Organize the center with bins containing a variety of 2-D pattern blocks (with simple designs to copy), magnetic tiles, and 3-D colored cubes, structural planks, and connecting blocks. Fill other shelves with games and picture puzzles.

In the photo at right, children arrange cylinder pegs by color, shape, and size.

Mini-Makerspace

Create a mini-makerspace for transforming, composing, and decomposing with loose parts, both recycled and natural. Dedicate at least one shelving unit or table to store these open-ended found and natural materials to provide children opportunities to create, read and write, cut, problem solve, build, connect, sculpt, mix, put together and take apart, make, and tinker. The emphasis should be on creativity while learning math, engineering, and spatial skills along with fine and gross motor skills.

Art Center

Add materials like molding clay, wire, recycled and natural materials, or loose parts and other 3-D materials to encourage children to change the shape and arrangement of objects by rolling, wrapping, twisting, stretching, stacking, and enclosing.

Cube Construction Center

Ask children to work in teams to build different constructions using five unit cubes. This is a great problem-solving activity. Challenge the children to find the twenty-nine different possible configurations.

- Each construction must be built so that it can be picked up, flipped, or moved in any way and not match any other construction.
- All cubes must be connected in each construction.

Jigsaw Puzzle Center

Offer a variety of picture jigsaw puzzles geared to the different interests and skill levels of children. Large floor puzzles encourage children to move their entire bodies as they complete the puzzle. Ask for donations from families and find freebies at yard sales to expand your classroom puzzle collection. This is one of the best known activities for enhancing spatial skills.

SPATIAL SKILLS AND VOCABULARY

- Compose
- Decompose
- Transform
- Rotate, turn
- Slide
- Flip

QUESTIONS AND CONVERSATION STARTERS TO EXPAND LEARNING

- What will happen if you turn this shape? What if you flip it?
- To get the puzzle piece to fit, what did you have to do?
- Have you found a way to put all those shapes together?
- What shape could you make out of these shapes if you put them together?
- Can you find all the pieces with a straight edge?
- What strategies did you use to find out if shapes were the same or different?
- How many different ways can you arrange those shapes?
- Which pattern blocks would you use to fill in the outline?
- How many squares make up your shape?
- How would you describe your structure to someone else?
- Can you tell me what's happening here?
- How could you cut this paper to make another shape?
- Can you make a shape out of this pipe cleaner?

EXPERIENTIAL ACTIVITIES TO TRY AT HOME

- Encourage parents to provide a variety of jigsaw puzzles, starting with simple puzzles for beginners and adding more complex puzzles for experienced children.

- Suggest open-ended play explorations using recycled materials from around the house, natural materials collected from outdoors, or inexpensive materials purchased from dollar or craft stores that offer children the opportunity to manipulate and transform materials.
- Unit blocks are available through school catalogs and online suppliers. While they can be costly, they are an excellent investment, lasting for generations.
- Some parks provide life-sized construction materials for families.

- Recommend replacing screen time with simple construction games. While they wait for her doctor's checkup, Charlotte's mother has brought along cups so that Charlotte and her friend can build various structures.

CHILDREN'S BOOKS: TRANSFORMING, COMPOSING, AND DECOMPOSING

Bruna Barros, *The Carpenter*
Samantha Berger, *What If*
Didier Boursin, *Folding for Fun: Origami for Ages 4 and Up*
Deborah Freedman, *This House, Once*
Michael Hall, *Perfect Square*
Grace Maccarone, *Three Pigs, One Wolf, and Seven Magic Shapes*
John Montroll, *Easy Origami Animals*
Barney Saltzberg, *Beautiful Oops*
Nancy Elizabeth Wallace, *Look! Look! Look! At Sculpture*
Ursus Wehrli, *Tidying Up Art*

Visualization and Visual-Spatial Working Memory

Spatial visualization is a type of spatial thinking in which we use the imagination to "generate, retain, retrieve, and transform" visual images (Lohman in Ontario Ministry 2014, 9). It allows a person to see complex patterns, understand and analyze visual information, solve problems using visual reasoning, and understand how things take up space and move through space. Mental rotation, a specific example of visualization, is defined as the ability to rapidly and accurately rotate two-dimensional and three-dimensional shapes in the mind without physically seeing or touching them (Moss et al. 2016).

Visualization Example

- Imagine that you have three green cubes, three orange cubes, and one yellow cube.
- Take all three green cubes and make a tower.
- Take all three orange cubes and make a tower.
- Take the orange tower, turn it on its side, and place it on top of the green tower.
- You should have a shape that looks like a capital "T."
- Now take the one yellow cube and place it on top of the middle orange cube.

- Take this shape and flip it upside down.
- Can you picture the 3-D object you have built in your mind? Is it A, B or C?

A   B   C

Answer: If you chose C, you are correct!

Going back to the time of Piaget, research on mental rotation indicated that children did not develop this ability until they were between seven and ten years of age. However, modern studies have shown that these abilities emerge around age four or five, suggesting that there is much we can do to support young children's mental rotation skills (Newcombe and Frick 2010).

Visualization skills are used in many of the activities suggested in other chapters of this book, but an emphasis on specific experiences to hone this skill is featured here because it receives so little attention in the early childhood curriculum. According to the Ontario Ministry of Education's report, spatial visualization skills are known to be responsible for big ideas such as "the discovery of the structure of DNA, the theory of relativity and the invention of the motor" (2014, 9).

VISUAL-SPATIAL WORKING MEMORY

Many spatial tasks depend on visual-spatial working memory, which is the ability to hold and manipulate visual-spatial information in your mind. Research suggests that visual-spatial working memory plays a critical role in math learning and achievement, especially during the early stages of learning math. Tasks such as knowing which number is bigger and keeping track of items when counting are examples (Moss et al. 2016).

Visual-spatial working memory works in tandem with verbal working memory and reading comprehension (Ontario Ministry 2014; Moss et al. 2016). While it is important to promote strong spatial thinking skills in these playful explorations, spatial thinking is not a substitute for verbal and math thinking. We have to remember to address all modalities, since as Newcombe explains, "Those who succeed in STEM careers tend to be very good at all three kinds of thinking" (2010, 31).

Listen and Assemble

The activity Listen and Assemble requires visual-spatial working memory, both spatial and descriptive language, and good listening skills. Children work in pairs. The first child builds a 3-D structure with large colored interlocking bricks without showing it to the second child. Sitting with their back to the second child, the first child gives directions to the second child, describing how to build the structure. The second child listens to the verbal instructions and attempts to build the same structure. Afterward, the two children compare their structures. They need to develop common spatial language to complete the task successfully.

A variation of this activity can be done with a small group of children using wooden unit blocks, which makes it more challenging because the children can't use color descriptors. One child builds a 3-D structure behind a screen or barrier. The other children are asked to listen carefully as the child who built the structure describes how she positioned the blocks. They then recreate the hidden structure with an identical set of blocks based solely on this verbal description. This requires the child who builds the hidden structure to use specific spatial language in order for the other children to make an exact replica. Start with three blocks. When the children have mastered this, add more.

See and Make

In the See and Make activity, the teacher quickly shows a patterned card to the children and asks them to build the same pattern by stacking colored 3-D shapes with holes on a dowel attached to a cube.

A variation of this activity is called See It, Build It, Check It. It is played with magnetic pattern blocks. The teacher composes an image with 2-D magnetic shapes on a cookie sheet. Children are then invited to recreate the image on their own cookie sheet. At first, the teacher can make the design visible as the children work but then show each additional design for only a few seconds (adjusting the time based on the ages of the children). The teacher can then facilitate a discussion with the children as they hold up their trays to check for accurate reproductions of the original composition (Moss et al. 2016).

SUBITIZING

Being able to instantly know the quantity of a small number of objects without counting is called subitizing, which calls upon both visualization and visual-spatial working memory skills. Subitizing is fundamental to math as it "introduces basic ideas of cardinality—'how many,' ideas of 'more' and 'less,' ideas of parts and wholes and their relationships, beginning arithmetic, and, in general, ideas of quantity" (Clements and Sarama 2014, 10). These skills are the building blocks of mathematics, and they deserve more time and attention in the early childhood day.

Subitizing Cards

In this activity the teacher has a set of subitizing cards. A small group of children sit around the table with the teacher. The teacher shows a subitizing card for about two seconds. The children call out the number of dots on the card without counting.

In another activity the goal is to match subitizing cards and numerals. For example, children are asked to match a four-dot subitizing card with the correct numeral. A small group of children work together at a table to match the dots and numbers.

Make Tens

In the Make Tens activity, children learn about part-whole relationships, or how numbers are made up of other numbers. Set out tens frames with different numbers of black dots. Children use cubes to fill the empty spaces on the frames to obtain a ten, helping them visualize the number needed to make ten on the frame.

If you are an online subscriber to the Teaching Channel, you may have seen Miss Latimer's Quick Images lesson that helps children visualize number combinations (you can find it at https://www.teachingchannel.org/video/visualizing-number

-combinations). At whole group circle time, Miss Latimer shows children how numbers up to eight can be combined in different ways. She uses a ten-frame magnetic board with large colored magnets to compose the magnets in different groups, all adding up to eight. She flashes the board with the number combinations so that the children can see them quickly without counting how many there are. The idea is to help children become fluent in visualizing different number combinations, in this case all totaling eight. Miss Latimer gives children the chance to explain how they figured out the correct total after a quick glance and helps them understand that there are many different ways to come to the correct answer.

Dice Games

One way to let children practice identifying quantities at a glance is through dice games. The children in this photo are rolling dice to see how many spaces they should move on the hundreds grid.

USING SCIENCE AND TECHNOLOGY TO SUPPORT VISUALIZATION

Many of the playful explorations featured in this book contribute to strengthening mental rotation and visualization skills. However, when children have the opportunity to experiment with materials that have moving parts, it helps them imagine, think about, and visualize how objects move through space. Asking children

to imagine where things go when dropped can improve their understanding of gravity and motion (Newcombe and Frick 2010).

Children have many opportunities to use their visualization skills while exploring with ramps. They can adjust the ramp's slope to change the speed of an object and how far it travels while at the same time considering the characteristics of the object in terms of weight and size (DeVries and Sales 2011).

In the photo above, three preschool-age children use their bodies to explore the relationship between visuals and sound. As they step on a piano mat, a webcam projects their actions behind them.

Knowing how critical visualization skills are for children, we shouldn't waste another moment to nurture this important spatial skill for our future scientists, engineers, artists, mathematicians, and inventors of new technologies.

LEARNING CENTERS

Block Center

Offer ramps and different types of balls, cylinders, or wheeled objects that can be used on the ramps. Ramp materials include wooden or plastic cove molding that can be purchased at a building supply store or through most early childhood catalogs. Include supports such as beanbags or blocks (foam or wooden) to hold the ramps at particular angles. After children have experimented with different ramp positions and pushed various objects down them, they will often set up new challenges for themselves and continue making adjustments through trial and error. This is the perfect opportunity to use the cycle of inquiry (Chalufour and Worth 2004), where the adult helps children define a problem by asking clarifying questions during their investigations.

Children test their predictions about what might happen when two cylinders roll down the ramp toward the tower.

Dice and Dominoes Games

Throughout the year, rotate different dice and dominoes games in your math center to present challenges in subitizing with increasingly larger numbers. Large-sized dice and dominoes encourage big body play.

SPATIAL SKILLS AND VOCABULARY

- Visualize
- Subitize
- Ramp
- Incline
- Slope
- Angle

QUESTIONS AND CONVERSATION STARTERS TO EXPAND LEARNING

- What do you see in your mind?
- What did you see or visualize that helped you to solve the problem?
- There are five altogether. You see three. How many do you not see?
- Where do you think the ball will go after it goes down the ramp?
- How far do you think the car will travel if you position the ramp at this angle?
- Do you think this cylinder will roll or slide?

EXPERIENTIAL ACTIVITIES TO TRY AT HOME

- Let children hide an object and then give directional clues to parents or siblings using spatial language, such as "Look under the chair next to the kitchen table."
- Suggest a family math game that introduces the idea of subitizing using a five frame and counters, such as coins or other objects. Provide parents with a blank five frame (like the ten frame on page 89) and instructions for playing the game: "Start the game by showing your child the quantities 1 through 5 in the five frame. Put one counter in the first box and say 'one.' Now it's your child's turn to show one. Next, put a counter in each of the first two boxes and say 'two.' Take turns to five. Play the game again, with your child going first."
- Ask parents to provide children with tasks such as setting the table with as many plates as there are people in the family or guide children with spatial directions to put objects away.
- Suggest that parents play simple dominoes or dice games with their child. In dice games, begin with one die until children are skilled at knowing how many spaces to move without counting the dots on the die. Add another die when they are ready.

- Encourage playing matching games like Concentration, which is excellent for strengthening visual-spatial working memory. You can use a deck of Go Fish cards that have matching images. Place the cards face down in rows and have each player take turns selecting matching images.
- Recommend museums that provide activities that foster spatial skills. At the children's museum in the photo below, children place scarves into a wind tunnel and watch them go in, up, and around, trying to predict where they will come out. Parents use spatial language to describe these actions to their children.

CHILDREN'S BOOKS: VISUALIZATION AND VISUAL-SPATIAL WORKING MEMORY

Mac Barnett, *Sam & Dave Dig a Hole*
Michael Dahl, *Roll, Slope and Slide: A Book about Ramps*
Julie Dillemuth, *Lucy in the City: A Story about Developing Spatial Thinking*

Perspective Taking and Dimension Shifting

There are two basic types of perspective taking. The first is the ability to observe and understand people, places, and objects from different points of view, such as above, below, behind, or in front of (sometimes called "embodied perspective taking"). The second is imaginary perspective taking, which is the ability to picture something in your mind from a perspective other than your own (Moss et al. 2016). Young children engage naturally in embodied perspective taking in their play when they climb a tree or a playground structure to get a bird's-eye view of what's below or anytime they look at their reflection in a mirror to see the reverse image. Equipped with fantastic imaginations, children employ imaginary perspective taking anytime they pretend to be big giants ruling a planet of little people or tiny spiders climbing a web.

Studies have shown that strong abilities in perspective taking relate significantly to overall mathematical ability (van den Huevel-Panhizen et al. in Moss et al. 2016) and spatial reasoning ability, but activities that promote this skill have generally been reserved for older children. However, researchers and educators using the Math 4 Young Children approach observed that young children can develop their perspective-taking abilities and that they find the tasks engaging (Moss et al. 2016).

In Mrs. Ciemniecki's classroom, a house with furniture constructed by two girls is viewed from above.

Adding a mirror to the block area allows children to view their constructions from multiple perspectives.

DIMENSION SHIFTING

Imagining objects or amounts proportionally larger or smaller is one aspect of dimension shifting. Mathematically speaking, it's about understanding scale, proportion, and ratio. For example, when children create buildings to represent actual buildings, they are scaling down from large to small.

Children have recreated a zoo with blocks (see photo to right).

Spectators observe the shark tank from above.

Another aspect of dimension shifting is the ability to shift from 3-D to 2-D or from 2-D to 3-D. An example of this is when children build structures based on a photo, drawing, or blueprint (2-D to 3-D) . . .

or when they represent what they have built in a drawing (3-D to 2-D).

 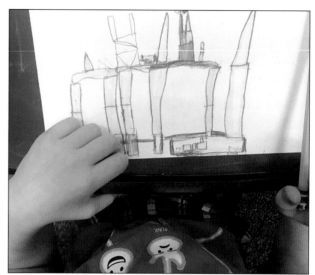

Clements (2004) states that when children have trouble grasping the properties of 3-D solids, it is possibly due to learning about them solely through workbooks, which are 2-D. He believes that children need more experiences with solids and more opportunities to switch between 2-D and 3-D with hands-on materials.

In the Make the Same Shape activity, each child is given a card with an image on it. The children then make a replica of the image using colorful unit cubes, which gives them the experience of shifting between dimensions.

LEARNING CENTERS

Block Center

Create an area within your block center with construction site photos, photos of children's constructions, maps, books, hardhats, notebooks with images of famous or local buildings, architectural blueprints and elevations (drawings of the exterior of a building from different points of view), and anything else you can think of to inspire construction.

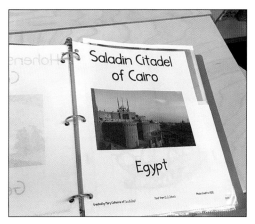

Lego Station

Create a mini workstation with interlocking bricks and photos of models to copy. Researchers have shown the benefits of following directions or 2-D illustrations to create a 3-D replica. In the photos below, Emerson is using Plus-Plus blocks to build a yeti. Picture directions provide step-by-step guidance for emerging readers.

Nature Center

Children can practice taking different perspectives while studying a flower. For example, children could draw a response to this question: "What would a flower look like to a bee or butterfly?" (Pollman 2017).

Math Station

Provide 2-D images of shapes and materials for children to construct 3-D models.

SPATIAL SKILLS AND VOCABULARY

- Patterning
- Bird's-eye view
- Points of view
- Perspective
- Two-dimensional (2-D)
- Three-dimensional (3-D)

QUESTIONS AND CONVERSATION STARTERS TO EXPAND LEARNING

- Can you draw your structure from the front? The back? Above?
- What do you see from the top of the sliding board? From under it?
- Can you make a 3-D model from this photograph?
- Can you draw your block construction?

- Does your structure match all three photos? From the top? From the side?
- Are the structures the same? How do you know?
- What would you have to do to this structure to make it exactly the same as the one in the photo?

EXPERIENTIAL ACTIVITIES TO TRY AT HOME

- Suggest that parents and children collect natural, recycled, or purchased materials to create a miniature fairy garden outdoors or a fairy house in a cozy indoor nook. This offers children new perspectives and a fun way to shift dimensions.
- Give families tips for using spatial language during travel, walks, or play. For example, parents can use directional words such as *above* or *below* when children are seeing things from different vantage points.
- To explore ideas of scale and proportion, suggest using blocks or recycled materials to recreate a smaller version of things they have seen or places they have visited.

- Parents can use a camera to take photos of places, objects, or buildings from different locations and angles and share them with children using spatial language.
- Provide ideas for setting up a table or floor area for working with interlocking bricks. Offer picture or written directions of models to copy (shifting from 2-D to 3-D). When children design their own structures, provide markers or pencils and paper (giving them opportunities to shift from 3-D to 2-D).

 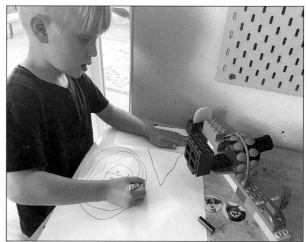

CHILDREN'S BOOKS: PERSPECTIVE TAKING AND DIMENSION SHIFTING

Niki Alling, *When I Build with Blocks*

Istvan Banyai, *Zoom*

Istvan Banyai, *Re-Zoom*

Julie Dillemuth, *Lucy in the City: A Story about Developing Spatial Thinking*

Neil Flory, *The Short Giraffe*

Pat Hutchins, *Shrinking Mouse*

Steve Jenkins, *Actual Size*

Anna Kang, *You Are (Not) Small*

Stuart J. Murphy, *Bug Dance*

Bill Peet, *Big Bad Bruce*

Esphyr Slobodkina, *Caps for Sale*

Chris Van Allsburg, *The Garden of Abdul Gasazi*

Walter Wick, *Can You See What I See?: Picture Puzzles to Search and Solve*

Spatial Orientation

Spatial orientation is knowing where you are and how to get around in the world. For very young children, it begins with becoming aware of the body and how it moves through space (Pollman 2010). Clements and Sarama (2014) say that moving oneself around leads to later success in spatial thinking tasks. They suggest that school environments, inside and out, need to include places for children to move their bodies, and teachers should include planned experiences to develop spatial orientation.

Teachers can make grids on the classroom floor using masking tape or by placing puzzle mats in rows and columns, then give children directions for moving their bodies on the grids. In this activity the teacher uses spatial language to direct the child to move on the puzzle mat. For example, they may be asked to move three units forward or backward, or move four units to the left or right. Children can also take turns giving directions.

Most early childhood educators know that the five senses of touch, sight, sound, taste, and smell are critical components of play experiences for young children. Lesser known is the importance of the proprioceptive sense, which is knowing your body position and where it is in space (Brillante 2017), also known as the "sixth sense." Proprioceptive ability is relatively stable by eight years of age but can continue to improve well into adolescence. Children with cerebral palsy, autism spectrum disorders, and other sensory processing disorders may have difficulty with spatial orientation (Tarakci and Tarakci 2016). It is important to provide all children the opportunity to participate in physical activities, even if they need assistance.

Active movement during play provides rich opportunities for sensory integration, an important foundation of learning both for typically developing children and children with disabilities. Newcombe and Frick (2010) believe that this type of active play has been shown to improve performance in spatial tasks. Activities that help children feel their muscles and joints working, such as digging in the sandbox, carrying buckets of rocks, reaching up to construct with blocks, climbing on playground equipment, and running, jumping, crawling, and squeezing all provide strong proprioceptive input in the brain, which enhances children's opportunity to learn where the body is in space.

As children move their bodies through space during play, teachers and parents have the ideal opportunity to teach positional language.

**Mrs. Krista Crumrine, Kindergarten Teacher,
Union City School District, New Jersey**

"This year in my classroom I have seven ELL students, six who speak Spanish at home and one who speaks Russian. Incorporating hands-on activities and language into all of our activities is an important focus for me. I also try to use authentic activities and visuals in any way I can to enhance the understanding of all my students, especially my English-language learners.

"I have included photos that cover two topics. First, position vocabulary: during this unit we did many activities using our own bodies to describe position and location, covering the state geometry standards. The photos I chose are of my class playing on the playground outside our school. I went around and spoke to students about where they were playing and had them use vocabulary and language to describe their location to me. Claudio told me that he loved playing inside the tunnel. Then he said, 'And look Mrs. Crumrine . . . this is me going through the tunnel!'

"I found Avivah sliding down the slide. When I stopped her, she told me, 'I was at the top of the slide, and now I am at the bottom.'

"Alisa tells me her favorite spot on the playground is to sit on top of the tunnel.

"For Alisa, who speaks Russian, these authentic conversations are so important. Alisa has been living in the United States for less than a year. Her language development is amazing and exciting to watch. Her confidence is growing each day with her vocabulary.

"Caley Rhonda joins Alisa on top of the tunnel. I took the photo from above the girls. When I spotted them, they excitedly told me, 'Mrs. Crumrine you are over us!'

"After returning to the classroom, I showed these photos to the whole class and we had a discussion about where everyone likes to play and the positions of all the students in the photos. The next time we went out to play, children were seeking me out to tell me where they were and to ask me to take their photo. We printed these photos and used them as a writing activity in the classroom to practice the words 'I' and 'am,' which we were learning at the time."

 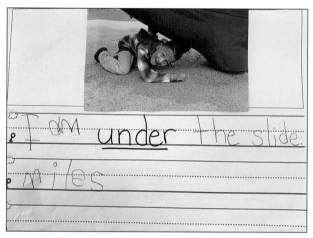

NAVIGATION AND MAPPING

Spatial orientation can also be described as navigation or "wayfinding." It is a different kind of spatial ability than mental rotation tasks, but possibly just as important in STEM and social studies as mental rotation (Newcombe 2013). Clements (2004) believes that having children create simple maps and build mental representations is important in developing perspective and the spatial skills of direction and location, such as left, right, north, south, east, and west.

In Mrs. Jarrett's kindergarten classroom, the children created a map of the school's neighborhood based on an online map that was projected on a screen. The children talked about where their homes would be located in relationship to the high school and other local landmarks. Although the image projected was an aerial view, most of the children created images and objects from a street-level perspective.

Mrs. Bhatia's kindergarten class created a mural of their neighborhood.

In the photo below, the children and teacher are sitting on the floor around a traffic carpet. The teacher asks the children to explore the places on the carpet, such as the school, market, library, and mall. She asks each child to go from the school to another place, such as the library. The child uses spatial language to describe how they will get there, including descriptions such as turning left or right, passing a landmark, or going forward or backward.

Young children need experiences to connect the physical world to its symbolic representations, such as maps and graphics. Kindergarten children from Çam Schools in Turkey were given the opportunity to see the relation between areas on the map and in the real world when they planned a field trip to the Pelit Chocolate Museum in Istanbul. Researchers Yusuf and Kevser Koc decided to turn this trip into an educational experience focusing on using visuals to support learning.

Dr. Kevser Koc, PhD, Associate Professor in Early Childhood Education, Istanbul Medeniyet University, and Dr. Yusuf Koc, PhD, Associate Professor in Mathematics Education, Kocaeli University, Turkey

"A map of Istanbul was reproduced for each child and a larger version was reproduced for the two teachers. The teachers marked landmark places on their way to the Pelit Chocolate Museum. On their way, the teachers alerted the children when they were approaching a landmark. While they were passing by a landmark, the children marked the landmark on their maps. The teacher showed the landmarks on her bigger map.

"After returning from the trip, the teacher and children discussed which landmarks they saw on their way and how they used the map. Additionally, the teacher asked each child to talk about the benefits of using a map.

"Since that trip, the children have been doing similar activities for every school trip."

TECHNOLOGY

Digital technologies such as GPS and Google Earth allow us to see space and spatial relationships in new ways. Interfaces such as interactive whiteboards allow us to manipulate objects in ways that are not possible with pencil and paper or chalk and chalkboard. This playful exploration combines technology, graphing, and mapping.

The children in Mrs. Bhatia's kindergarten class had been studying how to use and make maps in math and social studies. As part of their FOSS (Full Option Science System) science lesson on birds, they went on a hunt in the schoolyard to find birds. They were familiar with using Google Maps to explore their neighborhood, so Mrs. Bhatia printed out an aerial view of their school. As a class, they created a map key, which consisted of red, blue, black, or gray Xs. Each time they spotted a bird in a certain part of the yard, the children marked it on their map with the color matching the type of bird.

They went back to the classroom to discuss their findings. A few students shared their maps, which were projected on a screen. They noticed many birds were marked in an empty field-like area, which raised many questions and conversations about why the birds liked that area. A classroom display included the aerial photos with marks showing where the birds were found, along with photos and drawings of birds.

I have observed children highly engaged in a program called ST Math (Spatial-Temporal Reasoning, developed by the Mind Research Institute). ST Math promotes higher-order thinking skills. Children can visualize and manipulate objects over space and time with graphically rich, interactive programs that help even young learners develop deep, conceptual understanding of abstract math and geometry (Mind Research Institute 2019). The games can be played on an interactive whiteboard in teams or individually on computer monitors.

Children at the Boulder Journey School in Colorado are introduced to appropriate technology at a very young age. In this classroom, infants and their teacher explore the space between a projector and a screen. Three-dimensional materials between the projector and screen offer a means to explore space through physical interactions, which lends itself to a constructive and creative experience.

COORDINATES

In many classrooms today, coding offers another way to communicate about navigating through space, whether in the real or virtual world. In the photo to the right, three prekindergarten-age children work with a small codable robot (Ozobot) in a "robot city."

To lay the groundwork for coding, children can first be introduced to the idea of coordinates. Young children can grasp the idea of space organized into grids or coordinate systems. At first they may view a grid as a collection of squares rather than sets of perpendicular lines, but they will eventually see how they are organized into rows and columns and begin to understand that lines get labeled at points on the grid (Clements and Sarama 2014).

In the coordinates activity illustrated in the photo below, children match animals on the x-axis with ones on the y-axis, following the lines to move on the coordinates plane.

LEARNING CENTERS

Block Center

The block center is one of the best places to offer a variety of 3-D blocks, books, blueprints, and maps. Two- and three-dimensional transparent blocks can be used on a light table or overhead projector, which can be found in many school supplies catalogs. You could also provide two-dimensional images or books that children can recreate in three dimensions.

"Can You Make a Map?" Center

Create a map center that includes a basket with a checklist and materials for making a map. Collect a variety of maps, including globes, for children to explore.

"Outer Space Game"

For this game, you will need stars made from white or yellow card stock (laminated, if possible), with an action written on each (include a picture for nonreaders) with a label "alone" or "partner." You will also need a beanbag (this can be in the shape of a planet or moon to keep with the theme, but a generic beanbag is fine). The action should include spatial language, such as "(Partner) Place the beanbag behind your partner," "(Alone) Hop backward," "(Alone) Put

A basket filled with map parts and a list of features encourages children to build a 3-D map before creating it in 2-D.

the beanbag on your left shoulder," "(Partner) Pass the beanbag back and forth." You can create the actions or invite the children to generate them in a small- or whole-group activity. Create a game board using a clean pizza box painted black with the outline (in white or yellow) of ten stars the same size as the action cards. You can store the cards and beanbag in the box. You are ready to play the game!

1. Players take turns selecting a star card with actions.
2. The player performs the action according to the instructions, alone or with a partner.
3. After the action is successfully completed, the player places the card on the star outline on the game board.
4. When all ten stars on the board are filled, the game is over. Everyone is a winner!

SPATIAL SKILLS AND VOCABULARY

- Narrow
- Wide
- Forward
- Left and right
- Enter, entrance
- Exit
- Dead end
- Turn
- Straight
- Behind
- In front of
- In back of
- Side

QUESTIONS AND CONVERSATION STARTERS TO EXPAND LEARNING

- What landmarks did you pass on the way from your home to school?
- Should I turn left or right at the end of the street if we want to go to the park?
- Looking at the map of the playground, is the slide beside or behind the sandbox?
- Did you go over the tunnel or through the tunnel?
- How did you get your robot to follow the path?

EXPERIENTIAL ACTIVITIES TO TRY AT HOME

- Provide a list of books with rich visual spatial language and encourage parents to read them with their children.
- Suggest that families play familiar games like Simon Says or make up their own words to familiar tunes to help children learn to follow spatial directions such as left and right or up and down.
- Invite parents to create maps of a favorite playground space. Include landmarks such as the slide, swing, sandbox, and so forth. Another variation is to create a treasure map with pictorial symbols for landmarks and have children dig up the buried treasure, using the map as a guide.
- Recommend using spatial language on nature walks, for example, "Let's walk over the bridge"; "Walk between the tree trunks"; "Climb up the mountain."

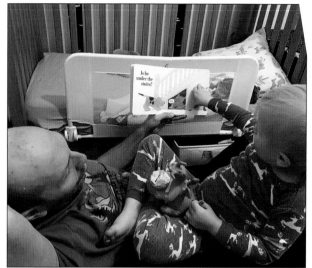

CHILDREN'S BOOKS: SPATIAL ORIENTATION

Katherine Ayers, *Up, Down, and Around*

Molly Bang, *Yellow Ball*

Neil Chesanow, *Where Do I Live?*

James Dean, *Pete the Cat and the Treasure Map*

Julie Dillemuth, *Lucy in the City: A Story about Developing Spatial Thinking Skills*

Julie Dillemuth, *Mapping My Day*

David Elliot, *Henry's Map*

Sue Farrell, *To the Post Office with Mama*

Gail Hartman, *As the Crow Flies: A First Book of Maps*

Joyce Hesselberth, *Mapping Sam, A Book about What Is Where and How to Get from Here to There*

Eric Hill, *Where's Spot?*

Tana Hoban, *All about Where*

Tana Hoban, *Over, Under and Through and Other Spatial Concepts*

Pat Hutchins, *Rosie's Walk*

Ann Jonas, *Round Trip*

Loreen Leedy, *Mapping Penny's World*

Alice McLerran, *Roxaboxen*

Bruce McMillan, *Becca Backward, Becca Frontward*

Akiko Miyakoshi, *The Way Home in the Night*

Stuart J. Murphy, *Bug Dance and Best Bug Parade*

Laura Murray, *The Gingerbread Man Loose at the Zoo*

Tish Rabe, *There's a Map on My Lap! All about Maps*

Scot Ritchie, *Follow That Map! A First Book of Mapping Skills*

Esphyr Slobodkina, *Caps for Sale*

Irene Smalls, *Jonathan and His Mommy*

Mo Willems, *Knuffle Bunny: A Cautionary Tale*

Gene Zion, *Harry, the Dirty Dog*

Visual
Representation

Researchers at the Center for Spatial Studies in Santa Barbara, California, believe that using images and "thinking spatially opens the eye and mind to new connections, new questions, and new answers," and these new connections enable us to understand the bigger picture better (Ontario Ministry 2014, 5). In this chapter we will take a closer look at how visual representations such as displays of data, drawing, documentation, and reflection open new pathways to developing spatial skills.

USING VISUALS TO SUPPORT LEARNING

Visual displays such as graphs and Venn diagrams offer a conceptual way for children to learn math (Boaler 2016; Schwartz 2017; Newcombe 2013). Two examples found in many classrooms are the number line, which provides useful spatial representations of quantities and their relationships (Ontario Ministry 2014), and a daily schedule with images to help nonreaders better understand the general flow of the day and anticipate what comes next.

In the next group of photos, Mrs. Crumrine's class is preparing to make applesauce. Each child brings one apple to school. Working in groups during this activity, the children complete a recipe, a type of informational writing piece, titled "How to Make Applesauce." Before they begin to wash and cut the apples, the children examine them. They count and graph how many of each color apple they have. Next, the children weigh and measure their apples using a balance scale and Unifix Cubes. In small groups they predict which child has the heaviest and lightest apple. They use the balance to compare and check their predictions. After weighing, measuring, and graphing the apples, they wash them, cut them, and cook them in a Crock-Pot. The following day they mash the cooked apples in a food mill and enjoy a delicious snack.

Joseph measures the height of his apple.

Avivah and Henry check their prediction that Avivah's apple is the heaviest in the whole class.

Mrs. Crumrine uses a chart and graph to visually communicate responses to questions.

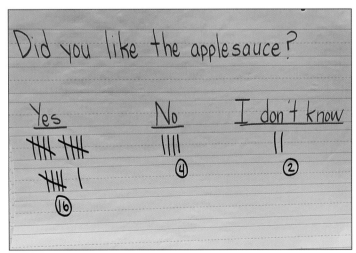

Investigating length, quantity, and volume conceptually with concrete materials is especially powerful in helping young children visually understand concepts such as bigger or smaller and taller or shorter.

In this preschool classroom, the children are measured for height at the beginning of the year with a length of yarn and then measured again at the end of the year. With the teacher, they compare the two lengths of yarn to see how much they have grown!

During dramatic play, Liam invites the teacher to the gardening store. The teacher asks if she can buy a pair of gardening gloves. Liam finds two pairs of gloves and compares each to the teacher's hand to see which size fits.

Many children benefit from using a wide range of visuals to support learning in other subject areas beyond math, like social studies, geography, and science. Offering visual references and images on any topic you are studying will support deeper understanding. In her book *Picture Science: Using Digital Photography to Teach Young Children,* Carla Neumann-Hinds (2007) explains that photography is an excellent tool for teaching science. For example, rather than using just words, showing photographs of the stages of a monarch caterpillar, from egg to chrysalis, makes it easier for children to comprehend the life cycle, especially when actual observation is not possible.

COMMUNICATING THROUGH DRAWING

Drawing is a powerful tool used by mathematicians, engineers, scientists, architects, and technical graphic artists, who rely on their representational skills to create and read blueprints, maps, and diagrams (Erikson Institute 2017). Sheryl Sorby (1999), an engineering educator, suggests that an important key to enhancing spatial skills is to have students sketch, or do quick drawings, from concrete models they can actually touch and see. This activity stimulates the "perceiving" portions of their brain more than working with 3-D computer models. Similarly, many artists sketch when studying a particular subject or planning a work of art.

Myra Fernandes, Jeffrey Wammes, and Melissa Meade, experts in the science of memory, conducted experiments to find out which activities help students remember information. They found that even when students weren't skilled artists, those who drew information remembered twice as much as when they wrote it. The researchers explained that drawing taps into visual, kinesthetic, and linguistic areas of the brain, so the information is processed in three different ways and therefore establishes more neural connections for deeper learning (Terada 2019).

Representation plays a key role in science education, promoting children's inquiry and science understandings (Chalufour and Worth 2004). Nora Newcombe, advisory board member of the Spatial Intelligence and Learning Center, which is funded by the National Science Foundation, explains that scientists often draw during their observations. Per Newcombe (2013), research shows that drawing enhances engagement, deepens understanding, and helps make ideas more explicit. For example, children can draw observations of leaves, make creations with the leaves, and check visual charts and books to identify and accurately label the leaves.

OBSERVATIONAL DRAWING

Children draw to make sense of their world and don't usually need much encouragement to express their imaginative ideas. Observational drawings are a little different, though, because they require you to draw something while carefully looking at it. In the photo below, children draw objects in the classroom. The drawings will then be posted on a large rectangular sheet of paper to make a classroom map. The children will then use the map to practice spatial positioning and language.

Here are a few strategies for supporting children's observational drawing.

Providing Materials

Provide an assortment of drawing instruments, such as pencils, black fine-line markers, and colored markers and pencils. Very young children or children who are still developing drawing skills can start with crayons, but older, more experienced children need a finer point to make more detailed drawings. Children can draw anywhere—at a table, on the floor, at easels, or at a light table—but attaching unlined white drawing paper to a clipboard allows for portability as children move between centers and indoors and outdoors. Ask for clean recycled paper donations or purchase inexpensive drawing paper or newsprint to encourage drawing throughout the day without worrying about waste. You can use better quality paper for projects when you want to add chalk or paint to the drawing outlines.

Deciding What to Draw

Drawing block structures is an excellent way to reinforce spatial skills. Show children where you have placed the drawing instruments and clipboard with paper in the block area, and invite them to draw their completed structure as a way to preserve what they have built before they have to dismantle it. If blocks don't motivate children to draw, remember that drawing any subject of interest—flowers, bugs, vehicles, or everyday objects—is still important in developing spatial skills. Help children notice the shapes and patterns in the object. You can even offer a magnifying glass for smaller objects.

Guiding and Responding

Keep in mind what you learned in chapter 8 about dimension shifting. Drawing 3-D objects helps children learn to shift from 3-D to 2-D. You might start with demonstrating how to draw a block structure, beginning with noticing and naming the shapes you see, and explaining how to draw the outline of each shape. Encourage the children to slow down, take their time, and really look at what they are seeing, paying attention to drawing objects in relationship to one another as they think about size and scale. If children get frustrated drawing a complex block structure, you might instead select one or two block shapes for them to draw.

While you want to encourage children to get better at representing objects accurately, remember to appreciate that everyone sees things differently and that each drawing will be unique. It is also important to understand that each child may be at a different stage of development in their drawing. You might notice that some children with language delays and those who are just learning English are excellent communicators through drawing. Even if children's motor abilities are not fully developed, remind them that their skills will improve with practice. Explain that just as you have to practice riding a bike to get good at it, you will get better at drawing if you practice every day. This should help prevent frustration and help children take pleasure in the process.

Although you don't have to say or ask anything as children are drawing, you may want to comment on details you notice or take photos to show that you value their efforts. Just being close and watching and listening with genuine interest is more encouraging and meaningful than a well-intentioned "It's beautiful. Good work!"

Guiding Children's Drawing

Use correct terms. "I see you drew diagonal and horizontal lines." "Can you show me the rectangular shapes you included in your drawing?"

Encourage children to reflect on their drawing experience. "Which part did you enjoy drawing most? "Which parts were hardest to draw?"

Ask open-ended questions. "Can you describe the difference between a symmetrical pattern and a radial pattern?" "Can you tell me about. . . ?"

Focus children's attention on the way they use art media. "I see you used the tip of your marker to draw curvy, zigzag, and dotted lines."

Label the child's actions. "I noticed that you were carefully looking at the insect you were drawing. You included so many details."

Introduce new art concepts with actions. "You made a three-dimensional model of the dog by looking at the two-dimensional illustration from the book."

Verbalize a problem and help children find a solution. "You made the petals of the flower round. Look closely and notice if the shape of the petal is round or more like a skinny oval."

Encourage children to discuss and arrive at solutions to problems. "Your group mural of the cityscape has some buildings upside down and some sideways. What can we do to make all the buildings go in the same direction?"

Encourage children to talk about their drawings. At circle time the teacher invites a group of children to describe what they each contributed to their drawing of the neighborhood, encouraging directional language.

Share drawing experiences and techniques. Encourage children to describe the process they used to make their drawings look three-dimensional.

Listen carefully to private speech. Listen to what children are saying when they are thinking out loud. Are they demonstrating an understanding of spatial terms and language?

Give children firsthand experiences to develop spatial concepts through drawing. After the teacher reads the book *Zoom* as inspiration, the children go outside to draw the playground from up close and far away.

Talk with children about artists from a variety of cultures and countries. The children visit the art museum to see the Japanese tearoom. The children return to draw a floor plan of the tearoom, then construct the tearoom out of natural materials and bamboo.

Invite artists, architects, engineers, and other professionals or parents to share how they use drawing in their work. An architect from the university shows children the blueprint of the new children's center and his sketches of what the outside of the building will look like.

Make connections between and among concepts. The children draw the different stages of the life cycle of the butterfly from photos they took.

Adapted for developing spatial skills from The Colors of Learning: Integrating the Visual Arts into the Early Childhood Curriculum *by Rosemary Althouse, Margaret H. Johnson, and Sharon T. Mitchell (2003).*

You can also have children use photos, book illustrations, or their own drawings to inspire three-dimensional creations in blocks, loose parts, recycled materials, clay, or wire to practice shifting dimensions from 2-D to 3-D.

The sophisticated drawings of the young children from the preschools of Reggio Emilia have shown us that we grossly underestimate what children can do with adult guidance. As we stated earlier, this does not mean that we should replace children's creative visual expressions with more guided explorations in drawing. You should ensure time for both. If time is at a premium, the first thing I would eliminate would be coloring books or worksheets that have limited educational value and contribute little to spatial development. A quote from Ursula Kolbe, author of *Rapunzel's Super-market,* reminds us that "most colouring-in books are a bit like junk food—harmless in moderation but definitely not recommended for a regular diet. Why? Because they don't assist children in 'learning to see' or draw. They may keep hands busy but they rarely provide food for the imagination" (2001, 118).

VISUAL DOCUMENTATION

Documentation, or what I am calling visual documentation, typically includes samples of children's work at several stages of completion, photographs showing the work in progress, comments written by educators, explanations about the intentions of the activity, and transcriptions of children's discussions that provide insight into children's thinking and understanding. Early childhood educators in the United States have learned much about the potential of documentation from the educators of Reggio Emilia, Italy. Carla Rinaldi, one of Reggio's leading experts on documentation, describes documentation as a valuable tool for recalling information and for offering the opportunity to reflect, reexamine, analyze, and reconstruct the learning experience, but emphasizes that "listening and being listened to is one of the primary tasks of documentation" (2001, 83).

When visual documentation is displayed in the classroom, it encourages children to revisit the activity to reflect on and revise their work, stimulating their memories and showing them that their perspectives have enormous value, especially for children who don't have the language skills to express what they know verbally. Observing and documenting children throughout the day helps educators more fully understand how and what children learn and better appreciate their strengths. It is an ongoing form of authentic assessment (Maher 2020), one that I encourage throughout this book.

Upon my return to the United States after a visit to the preschools and infant toddler centers in Reggio Emilia, I was determined to implement observation and documentation practices in a preschool setting with a commitment to the quality and aesthetics that I had admired in Italy. In my graduate thesis, I wrote about the challenges and joys I encountered as a new administrator, eager to build trust and collegiality with staff while exploring the systems, structures, and time needed to support teachers in becoming increasingly more skilled at listening to children and making that listening visible through documentation as a way to improve practice (Hansel 2001).

The vision I had in mind two decades ago is a reality today at one remarkable school in Boulder, Colorado. Alison Maher, education director and teacher education program director, writes about the process of documentation at the Boulder Journey School (inspired by the educators of Reggio Emilia) as one that includes observations, reflections, and actions as part of the daily life of the school (Maher 2020). At the Boulder Journey School, documentation is more than the end product of an activity or experience; it is a process that is "dynamic and alive," according to Maher, and one that benefits children, families, educators, and the community (2020, 3).

Educators at the Boulder Journey School use the collected documentation to engage in reflective practice—woven into every day, not just during in-service days—as a way to examine classroom experiences and make adjustments to best support children's learning. Maher explains that in addition to being an authentic assessment of children, documentation helps "educators assess their teaching, including the various roles they assume within a learning experience, the design of the environment, their verbal contributions and their body language, the size and composition of the learning group and so on" (2020, 5). What makes this observation and documentation process successful, as I likewise realized many years ago, is the recognition that educators need the time, support, and resources to engage in this deeper cycle of reflection and thereby strengthen teaching practices.

When parents and members of the community have the opportunity to contribute to and review the documentation, they bear witness to the intellectual powers of young children. The Exploring Boulder Game is an excellent illustration of documentation that makes children's learning visible for children, teachers, parents, and community members. Preschool children at the Boulder Journey School worked on this project over the course of one school year, employing many of the spatial skills and components of playful explorations featured in this book. Here is their story.

Boulder Journey School, Boulder, Colorado

Room 11 Teachers: Amy DeWitt, Jaala Shaw, Jenny Haan, LizAnn Nelson, Meagan Arango

Room 11 Children: Aeneas, Alexis, Bennett, Brady, Caleb, Cyrus, Emily, Eugene, Hadley, Harlow, Jemma, Joey, Juniper, Kai, Landon, Lexi, Mackenzie, Madigan, Micah, Natalie, Nico, Oliver, RuiAn, Sven, Will

Pedagogical Support: Alex Morgan, Alison Maher, Jacie Engel, Jen Selbitschka, Sam Hall, and Vicki Oleson.

Community Partner: Growing Up Boulder (www.growingupboulder.org), an organization that partners with children ranging in age from birth to eighteen years to develop innovative, user-friendly, city design solutions that meet the needs of all residents.

The children in Room 11 developed a great interest in playing cooperative board games and even created their own games. When the Boulder Journey School was invited by Growing Up Boulder to contribute ideas for a child-friendly map of the area, the educators invited the children to create a game featuring a map of Boulder to combine the two ideas. They would create a game that included a map featuring places in the community. The children started their research right away. Families were consulted and shared their favorite places to visit.

Emily, age four, drew Boulder Journey School because everyone visits the school.

They traveled to different locations around Boulder to explore. As each favorite destination was visited, the children created symbols to represent the experience. They shared the responsibilities of drawing and adding color and used a process of voting to decide which symbols would represent each space. A 3-D video of each space was eventually integrated into the game so that players could scan a code to view the video of each location.

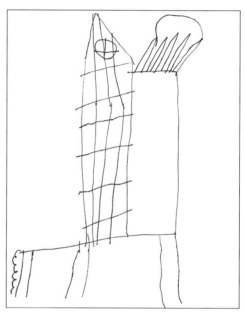

Rocket Ship Park

A kite store in downtown Boulder

Wonderland Lake

Next, the children considered the different contributions people make to their community. They compiled a list of important jobs in the city of Boulder, such as:

Plowing snow from the streets

Veterinarian

The illustrations the children made eventually became the task cards for the game.

Surprise in the mail.
Move ahead 3 spaces.

Garbage truck honks the horn.
Move ahead 2 spaces.

COMMUNITY HELPER

To play the game, the children created a game piece to walk, bike, ride on a bus or a horse, or fly in an airplane.

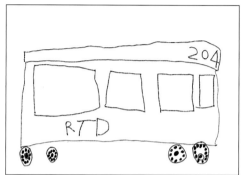

The teachers reflected on how to proceed: What was the objective of the game? In all the games we play as a class, even the collaborative ones, there is a way to win. Why else would you play a game? The children did not seem to have the same concern. So when the teachers asked about the objective, they were quite surprised by the answer. The teachers asked, "You know how in some games you try to build something or gather something? What do you do in your game?" Aeneas explained, "You go to the place you want to go." The other children agreed that the objective of the game was to explore. Lexi explained, "Yeah, exploring is like finding clues to what it is and where to find it." Now that the adults finally understood the children's intentions, the game was ready to be played by all, adults and children.

How to Play

1. Start at the Boulder Journey School symbol.

2. Roll the dice to move around the board.

3. When you land on a "Community Helper" square, pick a card from the pile.

4. When you land on a location, scan the code.

5. Go around as many times as you want, trying to land on each location.

From start to finish, the Exploring Boulder Game demonstrates that a playful exploration can be active, engaging, meaningful, socially interactive, iterative, joyful, and yet still be packed with plenty of opportunities for spatial learning. Using all their senses, the children moved their bodies in space to navigate through the local community. They engaged in dimension shifting as they converted their 3-D world to a 2-D map with symbolic representations of familiar locations. Teachers provided children time to observe the places they visited and gave them different options for communicating their observations, including drawing, painting, and language. Children and teachers made connections with community members and parents to inform their thinking. Ultimately, they invented a game that included a high level of collaborative problem solving. Children were so joyfully engaged in playing the game, they hardly noticed all the math and spatial learning that took place as they rolled the dice to strengthen their subitizing skills, counted spaces according to the task card directions, and moved their game pieces around the board. And finally, teachers created a visual documentation of this extraordinary, year-long journey as a way to reflect on each step of the process and share with parents and community members the deep learning that took place.

Ideally, our job as educators and parents is to give children ample time and support to experiment with and investigate materials. And in doing so, to marvel and wonder at what they discover, to assist them in finding creative solutions to problems, to encourage them to explore a variety of different ways to communicate what they know and learn, and, I hope, to appreciate and apply their newfound spatial skills throughout their lives.

LEARNING CENTERS

Block Center

Knowing what to build may be a challenge for some children. Visual supports, such as step-by-step photographs, can help children get started, but teacher guidance may also be necessary at the beginning. Collaborating with peers in the block center is an important part of the learning process. However, to reduce conflict in the block center and create more space for building, it may be necessary to limit the number of children using the blocks. Provide a visual reminder of how many children are allowed in the block center, and mark shelves with 2-D visuals to make it easier for children to return blocks to the shelves. Post photographs of children's complex structures in the block area to inspire more sophisticated construction. Provide a drawing surface or clipboards with unlined drawing paper and drawing instruments, such as pencils and fine-line markers, and encourage children to draw their structures when completed. This helps children shift dimensions from 3-D to 2-D.

Creation Stations

Create mini-stations at a small table or on top of a shelf where children can closely observe details and recreate what they see with 3-D materials. In the photo at top left, the teacher has arranged a small table with a sign that asks, "What do you notice? Can you create something with the materials?" Books about rocks and trees, a tray with natural materials, a container of colored pencils, and magnifying glasses are offered to inspire children's creations. Once they have completed their work, provide a clipboard with a sheet attached, asking them to reflect on the process by responding in writing to these statements: "This is what I noticed" and "This is what I created."

In another classroom the teacher displays a written prompt that asks the children, "What can you create from our nature walk?" and provides a book, children's work, and natural materials in bins or baskets on the shelves below.

Art Center

Enhance your current art center by offering a wider range of materials and providing books, visuals, and man-made and natural objects to inspire children to draw. Keep the art area supplied with drawing instruments, such as pencils, fine-line markers, regular markers, crayons, and colored pencils, and with plenty of unlined paper for drawing. Add colored construction paper cut into shapes, and have children glue the shapes into compositions on blank sheets of paper. Add a basket or bin in each center throughout the room with drawing materials and clipboards with unlined paper attached to give children the opportunity to represent their three-dimensional creations on two-dimensional paper.

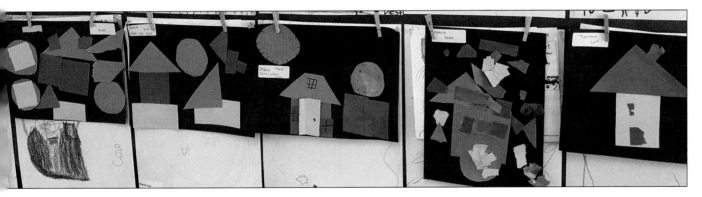

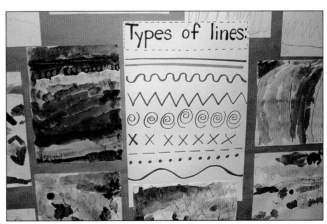

Light Table

Drawing on the light table heightens color and contrast. Offer a variety of instruments for drawing on lightweight paper (sheer enough to allow light to pass through). Add transparent or translucent shapes and loose parts to invite discussions and comparisons about the properties of materials and light.

SPATIAL SKILLS AND VOCABULARY

- Two-dimensional (2-D)
- Three-dimensional (3-D)
- Observational drawing
- Sketch
- Names of shapes and lines
- Rotate
- Turn
- Spin

QUESTIONS AND CONVERSATION STARTERS TO EXPAND LEARNING

- Which part did you enjoy drawing most? Which parts were hardest to draw?
- What shapes did you include in your drawing?
- Show me what part of your block structure you drew here.
- What can you tell me about your drawing?
- Is there anything else you would like to add to your drawing?
- Where would you like to display your drawing?

EXPERIENTIAL ACTIVITIES TO TRY AT HOME

- Recommend that parents create a mini art center with a small table and/or easel. Have paper available, and add containers for drawing instruments on a nearby shelf or attached to the wall to encourage drawing throughout the day.

- Suggest that parents purchase inexpensive sidewalk chalk for drawing outdoors.
- Provide parents with lists of spatial vocabulary, such as words that describe different types of lines and shapes.

ADULT BOOKS TO INSPIRE AND TEACH DRAWING

Rosemary Althouse, Margaret H. Johnson, and Sharon T. Mitchell, *The Colors of Learning*

Mona Brookes, *Drawing with Children: A Creative Teaching and Learning Method That Works for Adults Too*

Ann Gadzikowski, *Young Architects at Play*

Andy Goldsworthy, *Stone*

Andy Goldsworth, *Wood*

Ursula Kolbe, *Rapunzel's Supermarket: All about Young Children and Their Art*

Ann Pelo, *The Language of Art: Inquiry-Based Studio Practices in Early Childhood*

Mary Jo Pollman, *The Young Artist as Scientist: What Can Leonardo Teach Us?*

CHILDREN'S BOOKS: VISUAL REPRESENTATION

Adalucia, *The Magic of Clay*

Colleen Carroll, *How Artists See Animals*

Susan Clinton, *I Can Be an Architect*

James Dean, Pete the Cat series

Don Freeman, Corduroy series

Patricia Hubbard, *My Crayons Talk*

Barbara Odanaka, *Construction Cat*

Wendy and Jack Richardson, *Animals: Through the Eyes of Artists*

Chris Tougas, *Mechanimals*

References

Althouse, Rosemary, Margaret H.Johnson, and Sharon T. Mitchell. 2003. *The Colors of Learning: Integrating the Visual Arts into the Early Childhood Curriculum.* New York: Teachers College Press and NAEYC.

Berkowicz, Jill, and Ann Myers. 2017. "Spatial Skills: A Neglected Dimension of Early STEM Education." Education Week. February 16. http://blogs.edweek.org/ edweek/leadership_360/2017/02/spatial_skills_a_neglected_dimension_of _early_stem_education.html.

Boaler, Jo. 2016. *Mathematical Mindsets: Unleashing Students' Potential through Creative Math, Inspiring Messages and Innovative Teaching.* San Francisco: Jossey-Bass.

Brillante, Pamela. 2017. *Supporting Young Children with Disabilities in the Classroom.* Washington, DC: National Association for the Education of Young Children.

Byers, Anthony I., Elizabeth A. Cottone, and Claire E. Cameron. 2018. "From Design Copying to Mathematics in the Early Childhood Classroom." *Young Children* 73 (1): 80–85.

Center for Applied Special Technology. 2018. *Universal Design for Learning Guidelines.* Version 2.2. http://udlguidelines.cast.org.

Chalufour, Ingrid, and Karen Worth. 2004. *Building Structures with Young Children.* St. Paul, MN: Redleaf Press.

Cheng, Yi-Ling, and Kelly S. Mix. 2013. "Spatial Training Improves Children's Mathematical Ability." *Journal of Cognition and Development* 15: 2–11.

Christakis, Erika. 2016. *The Importance of Being Little: What Young Children Need from Grownups.* New York: Penguin Books.

Clements, Douglas H. 2004. "Geometric and Spatial Thinking in Early Childhood Education." In *Engaging Young Children in Mathematics: Standards for Early Childhood Mathematics Education,* edited by Douglas H. Clements and Julie Sarama, 267–97. Mahwah, NJ: Lawrence Erlbaum Associates.

———. 2019. "Children's Mathematical Thinking, Birth to Third Grade: Using the Learning Trajectories Tool to Teach Arithmetic!" Presented at the annual conference of the National Association for the Education of Young Children, Nashville, TN, November.

Clements, Douglas H., and Julie Sarama. 2014. *Learning and Teaching Early Math: The Learning Trajectories Approach.* 2nd ed. New York: Taylor & Francis.

Clements, Douglas, and Julie Sarama. 2019. "Developmental Progressions." www.learningtrajectories.org.

Copley, Juanita V. 2000. "Geometry and Spatial Sense in the Early Childhood Curriculum," Reading #34. Washington, DC: National Association for the Education of Young Children.

Danielson, Christopher. 2016. *Which One Doesn't Belong? A Shapes Book.* Portland, ME: Stenhouse Publishers.

Davis, Danielle, and Dale C. Farran. 2019. "Fostering Positive Experiences in the Math Center for African American Boys." In *Serious Fun: How Guided Play Extends Children's Learning,* edited by Marie L. Masterson and Holly Bohart, 67–81. Washington, DC: National Association for the Education of Young Children.

DeVries, Rheta, and Christina Sales. 2011. *Ramps & Pathways: A Constructivist Approach to Physics with Young Children.* Washington, DC: National Association for the Education of Young Children.

Dewar, Gwen. 2018. "Spatial Intelligence: What Is It, and How Can We Enhance It?" Parenting Science. www.parentingscience.com/spatial-intelligence.html.

Epstein, Ann S. 2003. "How Planning and Reflection Develop Children's Thinking Skills." *Beyond the Journal, Young Children on the Web,* September. www.naeyc.org/files/yc/file/200309/Planning&Reflection.pdf.

Erikson Institute. Early Childhood STEM Working Group. 2017. *Early STEM Matters: Providing High-Quality STEM Experiences for All Young Learners.* Policy Report. University of Chicago.

Fisher, Kelly R., Kathy Hirsch-Pasek, Nora Newcombe, and Roberta M. Golinkoff. 2013. "Taking Shape: Supporting Preschoolers' Acquisition of Geometric Knowledge through Guided Play." *Child Development* 84 (6): 1872–78.

Gadzikowski, Ann. 2019. "Architecture and the Hundred Languages of Children: Block Play through the Lens of Reggio-Inspired Practices." Presentation at the annual conference of the National Association for the Education of Young Children, Nashville, TN, November.

———. 2021. *Young Architects at Play: STEM Activities for Young Children.* St. Paul, MN: Redleaf Press.

Golbeck, Susan L. 2005. "Building Foundations for Spatial Literacy in Early Childhood." *Young Children* 60 (6): 72–83.

Gonser, Sarah. 2020. "The Spatially Gifted—Our Future Architects and Engineers—Are Being Overlooked." Edutopia. December 4. www.edutopia.org/article/spatially-gifted-our-future-architects-and-engineers-are-being-overlooked.

Gunderson, Elizabeth A., Gerardo Ramirez, Sian L. Beilock, and Susan C. Levine. 2012. "The Relation between Spatial Skill and Early Number Knowledge: The Role of the Linear Number Line." *Developmental Psychology* 48 (5): 1229–41.

Hansel, Rosanne Regan. 2001. "Visible Listening: Introducing Observation and Documentation in a Study Group as a Tool for Improving Program Quality in a Quaker Preschool." Master's thesis, Bank Street College of Education.

———. 2017a. "Blocks: Back in the Spotlight Again!" Community Playthings. September 5. www.communityplaythings.com/resources/articles/2017/blocks-back-in-the-spotlight.

———. 2017b. "Block Area." In *Big Questions for Young Minds: Extending Children's Thinking*, 19–23. Washington, DC: National Association for the Education of Young Children.

———. 2017c. *Creative Block Play: A Comprehensive Guide to Learning through Building.* St. Paul, MN: Redleaf Press.

———. 2018. "Guiding Children's Learning during Block Play." Community Playthings. October 9. www.communityplaythings.com/resources/articles/2018/guiding-learning-during-block-play.

———. 2019a. "Invitation to Play: Exploring 3-D Materials That Engage Young Minds and Bodies." Presented at the Early Childhood Summit, Pennsylvania State University, October.

———. 2019b. "Guiding Spatial Development in Young Children." Redleaf Press Blog. February 26. http://redleafpressblog.org/2019/02/26/guiding-spatial-development-in-young-children.

Hassinger-Das, Brenna, Kathy Hirsh-Pasek, and Roberta Golinkoff. 2019. "Brain Science and Guided Play." In *Serious Fun: How Guided Play Extends Children's Learning,* edited by Marie L. Masterson and Holly Bohart, 11–19. Washington, DC: National Association for the Education of Young Children.

Hirsch, Elisabeth S., ed. 1996. *The Block Book.* 3rd ed. Washington, DC: National Association for the Education of Young Children.

Jalongo, Mary Renck. 2008. *Learning to Listen, Listening to Learn: Building Essential Skills in Young Children.* Washington, DC: National Association for the Education of Young Children.

Katz, Lilian, and Sylvia Chard. 1996. "The Contribution of Documentation to the Quality of Early Childhood Education. *ERIC Digest.* https://eric.ed.gov/?id=ED393608.

Koc, Kevser, and Yusuf Koc. 2019. "Building Developmentally Appropriate Learning Environments for Effective Spatial Thinking: Understanding Learning Trajectories for Maps and Coordinates." Presented at the annual conference of the National Association for the Education of Young Children, Nashville, TN, November.

Kolbe, Ursula. 2001. *Rapunzel's Supermarket: All about Young Children and Their Art.* Byron Bay, Australia: Peppinot Press.

Kris, Deborah Farmer. 2016. "Can Teaching Spatial Skills Help Bridge the Gender Gap?" KQED. February 22. www.kqed.org/mindshift/43802/can-teaching -spatial-skills-help-bridge-the-stem-gender-gap.

Kuder, Brittany, and Robin Hojnoski. 2018. "Under Construction: Strategic Changes in the Block Area to Promote Engagement and Learning." *Young Exceptional Children* 21 (2): 76–91.

Lubinski, David. 2013. "Early Spatial Reasoning Predicts Later Creativity and Innovation, Especially in STEM Fields." *Science Daily,* July 15, 2013, Vanderbilt University.

Maher, Alison. 2020. *Documenting Learning: Process and Possibilities.* Exchange Reflections. ChildCareExchange. www.childcareexchange.com/catalog /product/documenting-learning-process-and-possibilities/8252513.

Masterson, Marie L., and Holly H. Bohart, eds. 2019. *Serious Fun: How Guided Play Extends Children's Learning.* Washington, DC: National Association for the Education of Young Children.

McClure, Elisabeth R., Lisa Guernsey, Douglas H. Clements, Susan Nall Bales, Nat Kendall-Taylor, and Michael H. Levine, with contributions by Peggy Ashbrook and Cindy Hoisington. 2017. *STEM Starts Early: Grounding Science, Technology, Engineering, and Math Education in Early Childhood.* New York: The Joan Ganz Cooney Center at Sesame Workshop.

McDonald, Patricia. 2019. "Observing, Planning, Guiding: How an Intentional Teacher Meets Standards through Play." In *Serious Fun: How Guided Play Extends Children's Learning,* edited by Marie L. Masterson and Holly Bohart, 21–31. Washington, DC: National Association for the Education of Young Children.

Mind Research Institute. 2019. ST Math. www.stmath.com.

Moss, Joan, Catherine Bruce, Bev Caswell, Tara Flynn, and Zachary Hawes. 2016. *Taking Shape: Activities to Develop Geometric and Spatial Thinking, Grades K-2.* Toronto: Pearson Canada, Inc.

National Association for the Education of Young Children. 2003. Position Statement on Early Childhood Curriculum, Assessment and Program Evaluation.

www.naeyc.org/sites/default/files/globally-shared/downloads/PDFs/resources/position-statements/pscape.pdf.

National Research Council. 2006. *Learning to Think Spatially: GIS as a Support System in the K-12 Curriculum.* Washington, DC: National Academic Press.

Nell, Marcia L., Walter F. Drew, and Deborah E. Bush. 2013. *From Play to Practice: Connecting Teacher's Play to Children's Learning.* Washington, DC: National Association for the Education of Young Children.

Nemeth, Karen. 2012. *Basics of Supporting Dual Language Learners: An Introduction for Educators of Children from Birth through Age 8.* Washington, DC: National Association for the Education of Young Children.

Neumann-Hinds, Carla. 2007. *Picture Science: Using Digital Photography to Teach Young Children.* St. Paul, MN: Redleaf Press.

Newcombe, Nora. 2010. "Picture This: Increasing Math and Science Learning by Improving Spatial Thinking." *American Educator* 34: 29–35.

———. 2013. "Seeing Relationships: Using Spatial Thinking to Teach Science, Mathematics and Social Studies." *American Educator* 37 (1): 26–40.

Newcombe, Nora, and Andrea Frick. 2010. "Early Education for Spatial Intelligence: Why, What and How." *Mind, Brain and Education* 4 (3): 102–11.

Ontario Ministry of Education. 2014. *Paying Attention to Spatial Reasoning: Support Document for Paying Attention to Mathematics Education.* www.edu.gov.on.ca/eng/literacynumeracy/LNSPayingAttention.pdf.

Pelo, Ann, and Margie Carter. 2018. *From Teaching to Thinking: A Pedagogy for Reimagining Our Work.* Lincoln, NE: Dimensions Educational Research Foundation.

Pollman, Mary J. 2010. *Blocks and Beyond: Strengthening Early Math and Science Skills through Spatial Learning.* Baltimore: Paul H. Brookes Co.

———. 2017. *The Young Artist as Scientist: What Can Leonardo Teach Us?* New York: Teachers College Press.

Pollman, Mary J., Rosanne R. Hansel, and Jessica Peters. 2019. "The Overlooked STEAM Skill: Creating Optimal Learning Environments and Experiences to Develop Important Spatial Skills." Presented at the annual conference of the National Association for the Education of Young Children, Nashville, TN, November.

Quenqua, Douglas. 2013. "Study Finds Spatial Skill Is Early Sign of Creativity." *New York Times,* July 18.

Rinaldi, Carla. 2001. "Documentation and Assessment: What Is the Relationship?" in *Making Learning Visible: Children as Individual and Group Learners.* Reggio Emilia, Italy: Reggio Children and Project Zero.

Rittle-Johnson, Bethany, Erica L. Zippert, and Katherine L. Boice. 2018. "The Roles of Patterning and Spatial Skills in Early Mathematics Development." *Early Childhood Research Quarterly* 46:166–78.

Sarama, Julie, and Douglas H. Clements. 2004. "Building Blocks for Early Childhood Mathematics." *Early Childhood Research Quarterly* 19:181–89.

School Reform Initiative. Retrieved 2019. Protocols can be accessed at www.schoolreforminitiative.org/protocols.

Schroeter, Edward. 2017a. "Part 1: The Importance of Spatial Reasoning and Geometry in Kindergarten." https://thelearningexchange.ca/importance-spatial-reasoning-geometry-kindergarten.

———. 2017b. "Part 2: Spatial Reasoning as an Essential Building Block of Pre-K and Kindergarten Education." The Learning Exchange. July 17.https://thelearningexchange.ca/spatial-reasoning-essential-building-block-pre-k-kindergarten-education.

Schwartz, Katrina. 2017. "Why Spatial Reasoning is Crucial for Early Math Education." KQED. January 29. www.kqed.org/mindshift/47269/why-spatial-reasoning-is-crucial-for-early-math-education.

Schwartz, Sydney L. 2005. *Teaching Young Children Mathematics*. Westport, CT: Praeger.

Sorby, Sheryl A. 1999. "Developing 3-D Spatial Visualization Skills." *Engineering Design Graphics Journal* 63 (2): 21–32.

Stipek, Deborah. 2017. "Playful Math Instruction." Webinar. November 1, 2017. Author's notes.

———. 2019. "Playful Math Instruction and Standards." In *Serious Fun: How Guided Play Extends Children's Learning,* edited by Marie L. Masterson and Holly Bohart, 54–65. Washington, DC: National Association for the Education of Young Children.

Strasser, Janis, and Lisa Mufson Bresson. 2017. *Big Questions for Young Minds: Extending Children's Thinking.* Washington, DC: National Association for the Education of Young Children.

Tarakci, Devrim, and Ela Tarakci. 2016. *Growth, Development and Proprioception in Children.* Foster City, CA: OMICS Group eBooks.

Teaching Strategies GOLD. 2016. *Objectives for Development and Learning, Birth through Third Grade.* Bethesda, MD: Teaching Strategies.

Terada, Youki. 2019. *The Science of Drawing and Memory.* Edutopia. March 14. www.edutopia.org/article/science-drawing-and-memory.

Topal, Cathy Weisman. 2003. *Thinking with a Line.* Worcester, MA: Davis Publications.

———. 2004. "Line Printing: A Process for Exploring Mathematical Concepts." Yumpu. July/August. www.yumpu.com/en/document/read/22938688/line -printing-a-process-for-exploring-mathematical-concepts.

———. 2011. *Explorations in Art*. Teacher's Edition. Worcester, MA: Davis Publications.

Topal, Cathy Weisman, and Lella Gandini. 1999. *Beautiful Stuff! Learning with Found Materials*. Worcester, MA: Davis Publications.

US Department of Education. Office of Innovation and Improvement. 2016. *STEM 2026: A Vision for Innovation in STEM Education*. Washington, DC.

Uttal, David, Nathaniel G. Meadow, Elizabeth Tipton, Linda L. Hand, Alison R. Alden, Christopher Warren and Nora S. Newcombe. 2013. "The Malleability of Spatial Skills: A Meta-Analysis of Training Studies." *Psychological Bulletin* 139 (2):352–402.

Van de Walle, John A. 2001. *Elementary and Middle School Mathematics: Teaching Developmentally*. 4th ed. Boston: Addison Wesley Longman.

Verdine, Brian N., Roberta M. Golinkoff, Kathy Hirsh-Pasek, and Nora S. New-combe. 2017. "Links between Spatial and Mathematical Skills across the Preschool Years." *Monographs of the Society for Research in Child Development*, 82, 1–150.

Wai, Jonathan, David Lubinski, and Camilla Benbow. 2009. "Spatial Ability for STEM Domains: Aligning over 50 Years of Cumulative Psychological Knowledge Solidifies Its Importance." *Journal of Educational Psychology* 101:817–35.

Warren, Christopher, and Nora S. Newcombe. 2013. "The Malleability of Spatial Skills: A Meta-Analysis of Training Studies." *Psychological Bulletin* 139 (2): 352–402.

Wehrli, Ursus. 2003. *Tidying Up Art*. New York: Prestel.

Zosh, Jennifer M., Kathy Hirsh-Pasek, Emily J. Hopkins, Hanne Jensen, Claire Liu, Dave Neale, S. Lynneth Solis, and David Whitebread. 2018. "Accessing the Inac-cessible: Redefining Play as a Spectrum." *Frontiers in Psychology* 9:1124.

Index